T0247759

THE COWBOY IKE RUDE

Nancy and Ted Paup Ranching Heritage Series

Paul H. Carlson & M. Scott Sosebee, General Editors

THE COWBOY # IKE RUDE

Riding into the Wind

Sammie Rude Compton

Foreword by Charles R. Townsend
With a contribution by Michael R. Grauer

Texas A&M University Press
College Station

∞ This paper meets the requirements of ANSI/NISO Z39.48-1992
(Permanence of Paper). Binding materials have been chosen for durability.

Library of Congress Cataloging-in-Publication Data

Names: Compton, Sammie Rude, 1945– author. | Grauer, Michael R., 1961–
    writer of supplementary textual content. | Townsend, Charles R., writer
    of foreword.
Title: The cowboy Ike Rude : riding into the wind / Sammie Rude Compton ;
    foreword by Charles R. Townsend ; with a contribution by Michael R.
    Grauer.
Other titles: Nancy and Ted Paup '74 ranching heritage series.
Description: First edition. | College Station : Texas A&M University Press,
    [2023] | Series: Nancy and Ted Paup ranching heritage series | Includes
    index.
Identifiers: LCCN 2023040288 | ISBN 9781648431777 (cloth) | ISBN
    9781648431784 (ebook)
Subjects: LCSH: Rude, Ike, 1894–1985. | Rodeo
    performers—Oklahoma—Mangum—Biography. |
    Cowboys—Oklahoma—Mangum—Biography. | Ranch life. | BISAC: SPORTS &
    RECREATION / Animal Sports / Rodeos | SPORTS & RECREATION / History |
    LCGFT: Biographies.
Classification: LCC GV1833.6.R87 C56 2023 | DDC 791.8/4092
    [B]—dc23/eng/20230921

LC record available at https://lccn.loc.gov/2023040288

Book design by Laura Forward Long

Unless otherwise indicated, illustrations are from author's personal collection

Page iv/v drawing by Don Stuckey

"One of the very few ropers, at this point in time, who combines elements of both the Old West and the New West . . . of both the old rodeos and new rodeos . . . a cowboy who loved to rope, trip, and tie steers and who probably put more right moves on more critters than any other 'tough scoundrel' that ever took out after 'em with a cluck and a cry. . . ."

—Willard H. Porter, "Tribute to Ike Rude," 1984

CONTENTS

FOREWORD

I am honored and thankful to have the privilege of writing the foreword for this biography of Ike Rude, one of my boyhood and lifelong heroes. Ike Rude's daughter, Sammie Rude Compton, wrote this biography of her father, a man whose life and career are so amazing that they border on the mythical. Ike stood five feet, five inches tall and weighed one hundred forty-five pounds, yet he could rope and tie down steers that weighed from seven hundred to nine hundred pounds.

Ike won three world titles in steer roping, the last of which he received when he was fifty-nine years of age. Almost seventy-five years later, his record as the oldest cowboy to win a World Title in rodeo still stands. Most authorities believe it will never be equaled.

As a teenager beginning my career as a rodeo announcer in the 1940s, I hoped but never thought that I would ever meet Ike Rude. That changed at the Washington County Fair and Rodeo in Akron, Colorado. On August 16, 1969, the first day of the rodeo, I went to the fair office to pick up my rodeo program for the afternoon performance. As I looked over the list of contestants my eyes settled on the name "Ike Rude." Later that afternoon I had the distinct pleasure of introducing him to the audience and contestants. Several of those cowboys were world champions.

When Ike, aged seventy-five, rode into the arena, the cowboys, some of whom were sitting, rose and stood along the fence as if to pay tribute to a true rodeo icon. Decades later my son Bill asked me how Ike roped that day. In the scheme of things, it did not matter. We all got to see a legend rope.

I always parked my RV in the infield of the racetrack that surrounded the Akron rodeo arena. Ike set up his camp about sixty or seventy yards from my camp. I walked up to Ike's camp, introduced myself, and asked if I could interview him about his life as a ranch cowboy and rodeo star. He agreed to come to our camp later that evening.

Around five-thirty that evening as my wife, Mary, was preparing our dinner and I was grilling some Nebraska steaks, I heard a horse behind me, and turned to see Ike riding up on his horse. It took him longer to saddle his horse than it would have taken him to walk to our camp. He was true to the cowboy credo: "Never walk where you can ride a horse."

We invited Ike to have dinner with us and he graciously accepted. I remember he sat next to me, took his hat off, and put it on the floor beside him. During the course of the meal, Ike asked if he could recite a poem. Fortunately the recorder was running, so that poem is preserved in this book. Our interview that evening lasted four hours, and much of the information gleaned that evening is in this book.

Just before midnight Ike decided that he needed to head home, so he mounted up and rode that long, sixty-yard trail back to his camp.

The next morning, I observed Ike as he broke camp, drove across the racetrack, and vanished into the fairgrounds. I watched until I could no longer see him. I never saw Ike Rude again, but I will never forget our time with him. Ike Rude's life and career bridged two centuries of cowboy life; he saw rodeo develop from its infancy in the nineteenth century to its maturity in the twentieth century.

I knew as I watched Ike drive away that morning that I would never see his likes again. How would I describe Ike Rude?

Cowboy.

Champion.

Gentleman.

—Charles "Bud" Townsend

Note: Charles Townsend retired as a history professor at West Texas A&M University in Canyon, Texas. For fifty-two years he spent his summers announcing rodeos. He was inducted into the Texas Rodeo Cowboy Hall of Fame and received an American Cowboy Culture "Lifetime Achievement Award" and an "All-Around Cowboy" Award. Townsend was awarded the 1975 Wrangler Book Award from the National Cowboy & Western Heritage Museum for his book *San Antonio Rose: The Life and Music of Bob Wills*. He also won a Grammy award for his album notes to *Bob Wills & His Texas Playboys: For the Last Time*.

PREFACE

Ike Rude lived a unique and exciting life as a true cowboy, a life that spanned the era of chuck wagon days, when he worked on some of the largest cattle ranches in the west in the early 1900s, to the beginnings of organized rodeo, which he helped to establish. He won three official World Championships in steer roping, or steer tripping as it is called today, but the title of the event wasn't changed until years later—after Ike passed—so I have chosen to keep my references to the event as "steer roping" in this book. He also won many large rodeos in calf roping and team roping. He always felt that he should have won about three World Championships in calf roping if the results had been properly sent in to the Rodeo Association of America (the organization that at the time kept records of all professional cowboys' winnings throughout the year), but many rodeos did not comply for several years after the organization had been formed. Ike also owned and trained some of the most famous rope horses in rodeo history. During his rodeo career, which spanned sixty-one years, he met and became close friends to a few other legends. I think it is safe to say that no one ever roped more cattle and had more fun doing it than Ike Rude.

My mother always wished there was a book written about Dad's life, even though there have been hundreds of magazine and newspaper articles, as well as chapters in books, about him. Once, in the 1950s, Willard Porter, a top rodeo writer, most respected for stating the facts, tried to do just that. He sent a rough draft to his publisher in New York. The publisher wrote back that they could not publish the draft as a nonfiction book, as they did not think their readers would believe it was true. The publisher told Porter if he wanted to resubmit it as fiction, then they might consider it. Porter wrote back and told them he could not do that as it was indeed a true story about his personal friend's life. Porter went on to write about Ike in many articles and books. He once wrote, "Ike Rude is a type that is fast disappearing and will never be replaced; a cowboy of the old school, a character, colorful, friendly, appreciated."

From time to time over the years, after Dad's passing in 1985, Mom or I would contact a few people who had written about rodeo, but none had the time or interest to write this biography. Time went by, and I realized there was no person left who really knew the story as I know it—as I write this it is the year 2022 and time to complete the record. I have stacks of magazine articles, newspaper clippings, book chapters, taped interviews, score times of the ropers at rodeos, and poems that Ike had learned on the ranches and recited over and over again throughout his life. These were all kept by my mother. They have been handed down to me. Of the "Ike Rude stories" that were told behind the bucking chutes, or wherever cowboys gathered, I do not have all of them, nor do I remember all that were ever told to me. A lot of these stories were told by cowboys long gone now, but some of them have been passed on to later generations. Believe me, there were plenty of these tales, and mostly all true!

The other day I went to the horse-training ranch of my son, Troy Compton. I was looking through the scrapbook of newspaper articles on Dad that I had put together twenty-some years ago, which Troy proudly displays in a room of memorabilia about his grandfather. I realized then that the ink was becoming unreadable on some. Slowly they are disintegrating. I have never written anything, but it is time to attempt this endeavor.

Ike lived fifty-one years before I was born. This book is written with much love to honor my father's memory and for the purpose of preserving a time in our history, of both rodeos and ranching. It is written with my best recollection of what Dad told me, the way I remember it, and also my research in the writing of others that I have accumulated. So, here goes …

THE COWBOY IKE RUDE

INTRODUCTION
A Brief History of Rodeo, 1870-Present

Circuses were a huge attraction throughout the 1800s. People who lived in larger cities were hungry for entertainment. In the 1880s, new versions of circuses, like Wild West shows, were being formed by people such as Buffalo Bill Cody. Buffalo Bill formed his first Wild West show in 1882 and toured throughout the United States with it until 1913. He even took it to Europe, where it was a huge success. In these shows there were staged gun battles between cowboys and American Indians, Indian dancing, all sorts of western antics and pageantry, trick and fancy riding, roping, and just about anything pertaining to the western way of life that might entertain an audience. Pawnee Bill also organized a Wild West show. The Miller Brothers 101 Ranch Wild West Show was another; it was formed in Oklahoma in 1905 and ran until 1915, then again from 1925 to 1931. There were others during this time as well.

C. B. Irwin was a cowboy who had moved to the Cheyenne, Wyoming, area around 1900. From then until 1911, he was the manager of the Cheyenne Rodeo and furnished the livestock there. He even won the steer roping at Cheyenne in 1906.

> 1912, C.B. and brother, Frank, formed their own Wild West production. Ringling Brothers was merging with the Barnum and Bailey Circus and they bought the liquidation which included grandstands, tents, wagons and various other equipment and supplies. By 1914, it took twenty railroad cars to move his livestock and equipment to shows throughout North America. He transported about three hundred horses, three hundred Mexican steers, running horses for relay and pony express races, and all equipment necessary to produce a show.[1]

After a few years of producing his Wild West shows, which lasted from 1913–1917, C. B. dismantled his production after his only son, Floyd, was killed in a freak roping accident at Cheyenne. By this time there was more interest in featured competition events. Wild West shows were becoming obsolete even though the folklore of the Wild West was still very much of interest to people who lived in the eastern region of the United States, as well as an attraction to people who lived in the West. A lot of the western people who lived this life wanted to compete with one another to see who were the best ropers or bronc riders. After C. B. Irwin quit producing Wild West shows, he continued, from around 1918 to 1921, to travel on his train with his livestock, some contract acts, and some cowboys to the rodeos he still produced. C. B. was one of a few producers who did in fact pay—though only in part—the contest cowboys (ropers and rough stock riders) who worked his rodeos. In essence, I guess one could say they became "contract cowboys." During this era, the early 1920s, he offered Ike Rude a job working at his rodeos for $100 a week and half of Ike's winnings. In return, Ike got to ship his horse, Blue Darter, for free on the train to compete in his rodeos. The cowboys that C. B. employed all got to ride by chartered Pullman, with their horses in the stock cars. The hired men and women had free room and board while at the "rodeos." Ike did this for a short while. It might have been during this time that Ike and King Merritt, another top roper originally from Oklahoma who had relocated to Wyoming and was also employed by C. B., became fast friends. C. B. produced many of the top rodeos at that time across the United States. He owned the famous bucking horse, Steamboat, who was a strong draw for his Wild West shows and rodeos. This horse is believed by some to be the bucking horse emblem on the Wyoming automobile license plates, but it can't be proven. C. B. Irwin was selling out performances across the country.

Prescott, Arizona, claims to have held the first cowboy competition in which cowboys were paid money, and it was held in front of spectators in the year 1880. Some other locations that have made the same claim are Canadian and Pecos, Texas; North Platte, Nebraska; and Miles City, Montana. Cheyenne, Wyoming, claims to have held a rodeo in 1872, but the first "Frontier Days" as we know it started in 1897, and became the first annual continuous rodeo. The rodeo at Pendleton, Oregon, started in 1910, Salinas, California, started in 1911, and Calgary (Alberta), Canada started in 1912. Since there weren't any legitimate records during this time, history cannot be proven as to the very first professional rodeo.

The early rodeos had few rules and were noticeably unfair competitions. The bucking stock did not have any eight- or ten-second rides. There were no bucking chutes—usually a horse was just snubbed down in an open area, or possibly an arena, and the rider got on. The cowboy generally just rode until they were either bucked off or the horse quit bucking. Judges were not trained or given guidelines on how to score a cowboy's ride. Cattle were not uniform as to their size and weight. Therefore, roping events were really won by "the luck of the draw." Bucking stock and cattle were often procured from surrounding ranchers.

Gradually rodeo producers and stock contractors were formed. These rodeo producers would bring their own bucking stock and roping cattle with them to the rodeos. Rough stock judges were informed how to score a good ride. It was the first attempt to try to make the rodeos fair by having somewhat uniform stock for the ropers to compete against, and a uniform scoring mechanism for the rough stock riders.

Others besides C. B. Irwin started producing shows and furnishing their own livestock. In the year 1918, Tex Austin produced the first "indoor" rodeo in Wichita, Kansas. From 1918 to 1934, he produced several "large attendance" rodeos throughout the country, but mainly in the eastern part of the US such as in Chicago, Illinois, annually from 1925 to 1929. In 1927, at Chicago's Soldier Field, the attendance was 350,000 paying spectators over the course of its nine-day run there. He produced rodeos at Detroit, Boston, and several other cities, including in 1922 the first Madison Square Garden rodeo in New York City. The rodeos featured trick roping, which was a judged event in those early years, along with the bucking and roping events. Colonel W. T. Johnson's first produced rodeo was in 1928 at San Antonio, then followed rodeos at Philadelphia, St. Louis, Chicago, New York's Madison Square Garden, Boston, and Detroit. Years later, in 1942, Gene Autry would start his own rodeo production company, which ran for a few years.

In these days, when rodeo producers started bringing their own stock to the shows, their mode of transportation was on a train. Most of the contestants, as well as their animals, were transported on these trains. Sometimes the cowboys, who competed in roping, would also ride the train, but then after horse trailers became popular, many cowboys would prefer to drive their own cars with trailers in tow, in order to take care of their horses better during long trips.

In 1926, professional men who were either producing rodeos or members of local committees that were holding rodeos attempted to form the Rodeo Association of America (RAA). It was a turbulent few years getting organized, but the RAA was finally officially formed in 1929. This organization had many problems to correct. Some rodeos that became members of the RAA failed to send in their records in a timely manner, and some sent none at all. It took much effort on the part of the RAA board and several years to get their members to comply with the rules. Without the accurate results of rodeos and recording how much money each cowboy had won, it was not possible to determine a legitimate world champion. This didn't change until later in the 1930s. By then, the RAA was able to properly tally the records of money won in a given event for the entire year, and therefore would be able to declare a legitimate world champion. Prior to this, many rodeos just advertised whoever won at the rodeo in an event was the world champion. The Pendleton Round-Up and Cheyenne Frontier Days were the two most important rodeos for steer ropers to win. Whoever won at these two rodeos was considered the best! In addition, rodeos had their problems providing competent judges and livestock of quality that was evenly matched both in the rough stock riding and the roping events.

Another problem was the lack of advance publicity of when or where the next rodeo was to be held. Also, never knowing how much purse money would be put up was a huge concern. The contest events were not well regulated, and could not be regulated properly by the RAA organization for several years following its establishment. A lot of times, the contesting men and women would get to a rodeo and never know if any money would be added to the purse. Many times, nothing was added. Only their entry fees might be put into a big jackpot, with that as the only money for which they would be competing, and nothing more! As determined by the individual rodeos, not by the RAA, at some of the rodeos the trick roping and trick riding competitions would garner the largest amounts of prize money; therefore the monies would not be distributed evenly to the other events. (In that era, trick riding and trick roping were judged events, not contract acts.) The RAA had their share of problems trying to get the individual rodeos to comply with their rules and regulations. Thus the purpose, as stated in part, by the RAA's bylaws read, "To standardize rules and events; eliminate unscrupulous promotors; to determine the true world champions based on monies won in sanctioned rodeos."

At the 1936 Madison Square Garden's rodeo, the cowboys who competed in the roping and rough stock riding were fed up with the way the sport of rodeo was going for some of the judged and timed events. The Garden's rodeo producer, Colonel W. T. Johnson, also had a contract to produce the Boston Garden Rodeo, which immediately followed the New York rodeo. The Colonel was not treating the contestants fairly: He was not giving them enough of the gate money that was being collected, the money still was not being distributed evenly among the various events, the cattle were mismatched and therefore unfair for competition. Hugh Bennett, a roper from Colorado, had been formulating an idea for a couple of years of forming another organization that would better represent the competitors and be able to enforce and represent the concerns of the competition cowboys. At the 1936 Madison Square Garden rodeo he presented his new idea to the cowboys. If he could get enough of the cowboys to organize, to go on strike and not compete at the upcoming Boston Garden Rodeo, they could demand better pay and better conditions. This would become the first organized strike that took place by a professional sports organization. By this time, Everett Bowman, an Arizona cowboy, endorsed Hugh Bennett's idea and agreed to be president of the new organization with Hugh as secretary/treasurer. So, in 1936, the Cowboys Turtle Association (CTA) was formed to represent the cowboys who competed in the judged and timed events. The name "Turtles" represented how long it had taken for the cowboys to "stick their necks out" and get organized and form an association. The original founding document signed by the Turtles is on exhibit in the American Rodeo Gallery at the National Cowboy and Western Heritage Museum.

From that point until 1945, the Turtles and the RAA worked together to standardize rodeo.

In 1942, the *Colorado Springs Gazette* of Colorado Springs, Colorado, ran an article regarding the RAA annual convention. In it, the organization discussed whether or not to keep having rodeos during World War II. The consensus was that they should be continued during this time as they provided such a "morale booster" for the general public. Also noted on the discussion agenda was the problem of contestants refusing to ride stock drawn in the shows or refusing to compete after arriving at the rodeos because of stock size variance. So it is evident from this article that some of the same problems persisted.

In 1945, the CTA changed its name to the Rodeo Cowboys Association (RCA). For a few years after that, the Rodeo Association of America joined with the National Rodeo Association (NRA) and changed their name to International Rodeo Association (IRA) until their responsibilities to rodeo were being handled by the RCA. Years later, the RCA would give Ike a Gold Card membership card, given to cowboys that had been a member for several years.

The pageantry around the rodeos included American Indian tribes who came and set up tepees for camping on the rodeo grounds for the duration of the rodeo events. Tribe members would perform dances both during and either before or after the rodeos. The early rodeos included entertainments of all sorts: parades, marching bands, bands playing during the performances, special exhibitions of all sorts of trick roping and trick riding, animal acts, quadrilles on horseback, and carnivals. This type of hoopla continued throughout the 1950s and beyond. The 1950s were referred to years later as the "Golden Years of Rodeo," as this era was when the glamour of rodeo was in full bloom. The RCA, by this time, was being run as a full-scale business. Promotion and the point system were perfected by this decade. After the 1950s, when trick and fancy roping had been converted to contract acts, and therefore were not being judged, were not as prominent, and were, in time, phased out altogether or minimized at a lot of the rodeos over the years. Women contestants were largely phased out after World War II. The cowboys did not approve of the cowgirls competing against them. In 1948, at San Angelo, Texas, the Girls Rodeo Association was formed for the women. The RCA started to include the barrel racing event for women at some of their rodeos. A few women still competed with the cowboys in various events at some of the RCA rodeos, but eventually the RCA made a rule that they would not allow women to compete against men.

In 1975, the Rodeo Cowboys Association changed its name to Professional Rodeo Cowboys Association (PRCA). The PRCA headquarters is at Colorado Springs, Colorado. In 1979, a hall of fame was added to the building that honors the professional champions and horses from past and present years. Over the years the ProRodeo Hall of Fame has had some serious challenges, including closing for a time in the 1980s and early 1990s.

The year was 1899; Ike was five years old. Sam Rude needed to make a cattle drive from Mangum to Woodward, Oklahoma, which was 120 miles away, or 240 miles round-trip. Young Ike wanted to go, but his mother was against the idea. Only after Ike promised that he would ride in the chuck wagon—not on his pony—did she finally relent. Yet once out of sight from

Ike, three years old, with rope in hand.

the ranch house, out came his little saddle from under the tarp. Ike untied his pony from the wagon, and climbed on him and rode horseback the rest of the two week trip. They had to swim the Washita and Canadian Rivers on this cattle drive.

Ike's idols were J. Ellison Carroll, who lived in Greer County, and Clay McGonagill of Monument, New Mexico. Both men were considered the best ropers in the country at that time. In 1905 a matched roping was held at San Antonio, Texas, between the two that required them each to rope twenty-eight head. Ike was eleven years old and could not wait for Carroll to return to Mangum to report who had won, as he was pulling for his hometown hero. Upon hearing that Carroll did indeed win, Ike was convinced that this was what he would do for the rest of his life.

From as early as the age of twelve, Ike was sent on horseback to the neighboring ranches to buy cattle for his dad. Ike would negotiate the price, make the purchase, and drive them back to his dad's ranch.

In 1910, Mangum held a local rodeo. Sixteen-year-old Ike entered the steer roping competition in his first rodeo. He roped off of Ol' Paint, a horse he had purchased from J. Ellison Carroll's nephew Frank Moseby. Ol' Paint wasn't of Paint breeding, he was a little bay horse with a slash across his forehead. He weighed 750 pounds, and the steers Ike roped at that first rodeo also weighed around 750 pounds. Ike threw his hands up in the air to make sure the timekeepers saw that he had completed his tie, and he won a day money at his first rodeo. (A day money is money paid to the winners of a go-round. A go-round consists of one turn for all contestants. Many rodeos have multiple go-rounds. The go-round winners are added together and whoever has won the most money is the "average" winner.) At one time a picture of this event hung in the American Quarter Horse Hall of Fame at Amarillo, Texas. The caption under it read, "The first man to throw his hands in the air to signal for time to stop." This action soon caught on with all contestants, and to this day is still used in steer roping and calf roping in rodeo. This same picture hangs in the National Cowboy and Western Heritage Museum in Oklahoma City, Oklahoma, blown up as a large banner at the Steer Roping display in the American Rodeo Gallery.

After finishing the eighth grade, Ike figured he'd had enough schooling. He would rather be working on a ranch, taking care of cattle, roping, and doing what he loved. In those days, it was common for boys to quit school and to go to work without attending high school.

Ike, age sixteen, steer roping at a 1910 rodeo in Mangum, Oklahoma, throwing his hands up in the air to signal for time to stop. His first rodeo.

The figure second from the left, hands on hips, is believed to be Ike Rude, age sixteen. *Some Matador Ranch Cowboys celebrating at the railroad yard after delivering a shipment of cattle, Lubbock, Texas.* 1910. Photograph by Erwin E. Smith. Nitrate negative. From the Erwin E. Smith Collection of the Library of Congress on deposit at the Amon Carter Museum, LC.S59.308.

Ike on Ol' Paint, 1910.

MILL IRON

Ike went to work cowpunching for the Mill Iron Ranch located in the far south part of the Texas Panhandle when he was fifteen years old in 1909. That year he worked on and off for them, as he was still completing the eighth grade at Mangum. Upon finishing school, he became a full-time cowboy for the ranch in 1910 at the age of sixteen. The Mill Irons had purchased the ranch from the Rocking Chairs, which were branding about 10,000 to 12,000 head of calves a year. The winter of 1910 to 1911, Ike lived in one of the dugouts on the ranch and took care of 2,000 Mexican steers. Ike recalled it sure was a cold winter living there.

Ike said that he never wanted to work for an outfit that wasn't a large outfit, and he didn't for a long time. The reason being if you worked for a much smaller cattle ranch, then they would put you to work doing other things like repairing the windmill, fence-building, or a jillion other things that kept you from being on a horse and roping. When his winter job was over, he saddled his horse and set out once again to find a ranch job (see appendix 2).*

Ike, seventeen years old in 1911, breaking horses at the Mill Irons.
Snubbed horse down, getting ready to step in the saddle.

*Note: For more history on this and other ranches in this book, refer to appendix 2.

TWO
The Matadors, 1911–1914

This time Ike, once again aboard Ol' Paint, headed to Tom Burnett's ranch, the Four Sixes (6666) at Guthrie, Texas. Tom, having already heard of Ike's roping ability, told him he had a job if he wanted it but work wasn't going to start for a couple more weeks. Ike decided to ride north to the Matadors to see if they might have work that would start sooner.

He landed a job there at the famed Matador Land and Cattle Company ranch, an operation in the Texas Panhandle that had about 1.5 million acres at the time and ran 12,000 to 15,000 calves. At first they were reluctant to hire a "kid" to do a man's work, but after Ike demonstrated his roping skills, he became one of the cowboys for the next two and a half years. Ike was paid $25 a month plus room and board. As quoted in an article, Ike said, "We had plenty of room—all the ground we wanted to sleep on—and the board wasn't too bad. We had beef and beans and sometimes beans and beef."[1] Other times there would be baked pies, vinegar pudding, potatoes and gravy, stew, and bacon and eggs, if the cowboys were near a town.

The Matadors had two chuck wagons. Each wagon took a wagon boss, a horse wrangler, a cook, and about fifteen cowboys plus around 130 to 140 head of horses with them on a round-up. Each cowboy was assigned nine to ten head of horses, each with a specific purpose: a drive horse, a round-up horse, a cutting horse, a night horse, an evening horse, and a throw-in horse (A throw-in horse was an extra horse to have on hand if one of the other horses came up lame or something else happened to cause him to be unable to be used). A cowboy would most often have more than one horse in each category. Depending on the job at hand, they rode whichever horse was the best at that job. The best horses were the cutting horses. Since many miles were covered during the day, the cowboys often changed horses to keep them fresh so as not to exhaust them from overworking. The horses

Matador cowboys, 1914: Ike in a black sweater (*seated, left*), John McMurty (*standing, right*), and Billy Partlow, known as "The Pitchfork Kid" (*standing, in back*). Billy won the steer roping at Seymour, Texas, in 1884.

Base camp on the Ranch. Ike standing in front of the Matador Ranch Chuck Wagon, weaing a black turtleneck sweater, with arms folded, 1914. Unknown photographer. Safety film negative. Rodeo Historical Society Records, Dickinson Research Center, National Cowboy and Western Heritage Museum, RC2011.004.

were hobbled at night, as there were no corrals. Of a morning, the cowboys would all help in getting the hobbles off all the horses in the remuda, as well as their mount for the day. The men would take the hobbles and tie a set around their belts to keep with them if needed during the day, and also to hobble them again at night. The horse wrangler would then be in charge of the rest of the horses that were not being used for that particular day. He would stay at the chuck wagon camp to tend to them. After getting all the hobbles off, the men would catch their round-up horse for the morning, eat breakfast, and were in the saddle by daylight. Days started very early. As Ike put it, "You better be ready to leave camp before the first crow left."

Sometimes a cowboy might stay at the wagon with the horse wrangler to ride some of the younger horses that were still fairly green (meaning not broke well enough yet); other times he might be assigned to go out and catch some of the lost horses or cattle (referred to as "back-prowling"), rather than go out on the round-up for the day. The cattle were often infected with screw worms in those days, and a lot of time was spent doctoring for that. The cowboys carried the medicine with them, but they would have to rope the cattle to doctor them.

Generally the wagon would leave headquarters around April and would not return until cold weather, sometimes not until December. On occasion, it would come back to headquarters around the fourth of July for ten or fifteen days if the spring work got finished, then the wagon would leave again for fall work. The ground was the cowboy's bed, and when it rained, if they were lucky enough to be close to any trees, they would put their bedroll under the trees for a little protection. When the weather turned really cold in the fall or early winter before they came back to headquarters, they had tepees they would put their bedroll in. Ike said those tepees worked really well. That must have been like sleeping in the Holiday Inn after sleeping for months on the open prairie!

When the wagons would leave out to make their roundups, one wagon would go one way and the other the opposite direction, taking the cowboys and their horses with it. At that time, the Matador Ranch was fenced into pastures. But don't let this mislead you—the largest pasture, named Turtle Hole, had thirteen sections in it, totaling 8,320 acres. Each pasture usually had a camp, with the smallest pasture being two or three sections. The cowboys would do their cattle drives, bringing the cattle together at a designated place to castrate, doctor, or separate calves away from the cows. Usually they would do their drives by the lay of the land, using designated ravines or rivers as landmarks while they were rounding up the cattle. Ike said, "Usually half the cowboys would go one way and the other half the opposite direction and then bring them together. Then usually the two wagons, cowboys, and their horses would join together with the cattle when they were to be shipped. The calves were cut, which means to separate, from their mothers at this time. Since they only cut the calves off as yearlings, sometime late yearlings, a lot of the mother cows would have their new born calf plus their yearling on their side." One sure needed a good cow pony for this feat, as this was all done out in the open without corrals to contain and control the cattle.

At branding time, of course back then there were no chutes, so they roped the cattle and drug them to the fire to be branded. All this was done with cowboys on horseback holding the cattle together to contain the herd. The "hoodlum wagon" would bring all the branding irons and equipment out to the branding sites. A lot of times these places would be quite far from the chuck wagon, so when they were done with their day's work, they would have to ride back to the chuck wagon to eat their evening meal and bed down for the night in the bedrolls, which were kept at the wagon. They would drive the cattle to either Paducah or Channing, Texas, which were the shipping points. Later some of the cattle would be shipped up to Montana.

The Matadors had thirteen camps. They were what they called "line camps" or "cow camps." At each of these sites generally one of the married cowboys would stay year-round with their family in order to take care of the cattle in their area when the round-ups weren't taking place. These were isolated and lonely times for those families. Sometimes in the winter months, cowboys would be sent out to these line camps to help out the man living there. In the wintertime the cowboys stayed busy doctoring cattle, repairing windmills and fences, breaking horses, and so on.

In the year 1913, Ike heard of a goat roping being held at Gem City, Texas. This was a little settlement just east of Canadian, Texas. Ike had not roped goats much before, but figured that if it moved, he could rope it! So Ike headed off to his first competition at goat roping.

It was during either 1913 or 1914, while he was working for the Matadors in the far northwest corner of Motley County, Texas, when he saw fifteen to twenty covered wagons going to New Mexico, where the people were going to take up claims. Most of these people were from back east, and when they saw the Matador cowboys washing their clothes at a windmill, the "to-be settlers" came over and quizzed them about their "wild" lifestyle and what they did on the ranches. The Easterners said they presumed none of the cowboys had any education since they lived this kind of life in the wild and wooly West. One of the cowboys who was really exaggerating and spoofing the group replied, "No, none of them knew anything. All they knew about was just a blasted rope and a pitchin' horse." Ike said the guy that was talking "couldn't have ridden in a covered wagon," meaning that he wasn't even good at riding a horse—he was not one of the cowboys who went on the roundups and roped and herded. This man's job during the roundups was to flank the cattle during the brandings, build fences, and work on windmills. Ike said, "He could sure flank calves good though, as he was a big guy." They all got a big kick that day out of telling yarns to the Easterners, who—in the cowboys' minds—were the uneducated ones.

Those cowboys were happy, carefree people, and were doing what they loved. Ike said the only one who ever had to worry was the wagon boss, and Ike never wanted that job. This was Ike's attitude all of his life: he never had a worry, was carefree and happy as long as he could rope. He never wanted to be in charge of anything, which would have been far too confining for his carefree spirit! They made up their fun as they worked. One time one of the hands had killed a huge old rattlesnake and he thought it would be a good joke to bring it back to the wagon and show the cook. Ike said that the guy came riding into camp with that snake coiled up on his saddle like a rope. He then threw it down at the cook's feet. The cook got mad and told him to get that thing out of there. The cowboy was riding a prancing horse that was tearing up the campgrounds and the horse was making the cowboy mad, so he decided to run the horse down to the creek and try to take some of the "prancing" out of him. Ike said that they saw him "over and undering" him for a long time, which meant whipping him on one side and then the other. Then he started running him back toward camp when the horse stepped in a rat's nest hole. The horse went down just as if it had been fore-footed. Fore-footing is a form of throwing one's rope so it catches the animal's front legs in order to bring the animal down. Horse and rider went head over heels in a somersault. The cowboys sure got a kick out of this escapade. Wrecks were excitement to the cowboys, who lived a rather lonesome life. They had to create their own entertainment

Ike could recite all the boundaries of the ranch and even most of the big neighboring ranches in the Texas Panhandle. There were no roads back then, so boundary lines were usually formed by rivers, streams, ridges, ravines, or cow trails. Working on these huge ranches, one learned a lot about the geography of the land while riding horse-back across it. Ike also knew many important landmarks as either des-tinations or meeting places when moving the cattle. Just as important was knowing the cardinal directions at all times to avoid getting lost.

Ike loved to rope, and he did so every chance he got, which was far more than necessary on the ranches. Any time a cow or calf would move, it gave Ike an opportunity to chase him and out would come Ike's rope. This was not the best quality for a cowman if you're a rancher try-ing to keep weight on your cattle. All the cowboys got to rope on the roundup, but were supposed to do so only if a cow or calf broke loose from the herd, to bring in a stray, when they doctored cattle, or when was otherwise necessary. But when Ike was off by himself and no one was watching, he would rope a lot. At branding time, generally just the "straw boss" got to rope to bring the calves to the fire. Cowboys generally did not get to rope just for the fun of it, as Ike wanted to do.

Once at the Matadors in 1914, Big John Jackson, the boss, was cutting horses out for his winter horses. He kept asking the cowboys who had been riding this particular horse. Always the answer was the same: "Ikey Rude." This went on for several more horses; the answer still the same. He was asking because every horse he asked about was skinned up from going through brush much too often. Another cowboy working with Ike had a lot of skinned up horses also. Big John sent Ike to Childress, Texas, to break horses as punishment. The other cowboy got fired. This didn't sit too well with Ike, so he quit. Ike figured if you were going to get in trouble for roping, he didn't want to work there and would go elsewhere[2] (also see appendix 2).

THREE

The JAs, 1914–1915

After leaving the Matadors, Ike rode back home for a short spell. He had a worn-out saddle and no money. For a few months he worked on some neighboring ranches and would ride his horse to nearby steer or goat ropings, always honing his roping skills.

In 1914, twenty-year-old Ike set out again, riding west. This time he landed a cow punching job at the JA Ranch, which was headquartered in the lower Palo Duro Canyon in West Texas. Ike was paid $30 a month, and again all the room you wanted and board.

The JAs were running a chuck wagon also, and the work was the same as Ike did at the Matadors. The JAs encompassed parts of Randall, Armstrong, Donley, Hall, Briscoe, and Swisher Counties in Texas. Ike said when they would go out on their round-ups they could be as far as forty miles or more from headquarters.

The JA Ranch was originated by Charles Goodnight and John and Cornelia Adair. By 1885 the ranch owned 1,325,000 acres. According to Ike, the old-timers told him that Charles Goodnight had acquired the land by running the "nesters" off with a Winchester rifle—he would tell them it was his land and to get off. The land in fact belonged to the State of Texas, but Goodnight bluffed. The nesters were scared of him, so they left. Ike said that he never heard of Goodnight actually killing anyone, but he did not know that for fact. There were no nesters in that part of the country at that time to confirm or deny the stories. Charles Goodnight did, however, run off the buffalo that grazed the prairie there at that time.

A few years after the death of John Adair, Charles Goodnight sold his interest out to Cornelia Adair. The Adairs were from England. By the time Ike joined the ranch, Mrs. Adair was the sole owner.

There were quite a few dances held at neighboring ranches and various towns for entertainment in those days. People would come in wagons and ride horses from as far as fifty miles away. "Put Your Little Foot," "The Cowboy Loop," and square dances and waltzes were popular. Two of the tunes Ike remembered that he especially liked to dance to were "Hell among the Yearlings" and "The Eighth of January." Sometimes the cowboys would dance with one another in the bunkhouse at headquarters. They even had stag dancing at their camps in the evening by the chuck wagon. Ike said, "We would kick the dirt up and looked like a bunch of jelly beans out there on the prairie." Usually someone could play the French harp or fiddle, and the cowboys would square dance with one another. Sometimes they would dance all night and be ready to go to work the next day before daybreak. Ike liked to dance.

One particular time Ike and John McMurtry, a hand who had previously worked with Ike at the Matadors, heard of a dance a few miles from their round-up. Being young and wanting some excitement, they decided to go when they got through with their day's work. They had to be back to camp before sunup the next day. They stayed a little too long, had a little too much to drink, and were late getting started on their way home. It was as dark as the ace of spades that night, Ike recalled. They were racing their horses across the country to get back to their camp when they came upon a barbed-wire fence. They rode their horses into it at a high gallop. The horses went head over heels, cutting up both horses pretty badly, as well as Ike and John. Ike said he hadn't known that a fence had been put up there recently. They made it back to the wagon in time to start the day's work, but they were two tired and injured cowpunchers.

Another JA episode Ike recalled was that Loy Cooper, who at thirty-five or forty years of age, was known as an old maid. Loy had been raised out on a cow camp all her life and was a very rough, tough, sort of woman. One day, not long after she had attended a dance held at the train station, she came riding out to one of the chuck wagon camps and told the wagon boss, "I ain't havin' no fun. Nobody will dance with me at the dances." The boss then ordered every cowboy there to dance with her that night. Ike said they liked to wear her out dancing all evening. He also related a story he'd heard about her: Apparently she had never had a dress on in her life. After her parents went to town and bought her a calico dress, she put it on and looked in a mirror and saw all that material behind her and she went to pitchin' and ran clear over a three-wire fence and cut herself to pieces.

Ike's buddy Henry Rowden, a JA cowboy. As Ike said,
"He could ride any man's horse."

Ike told this story during the taped interview recordings, saying he didn't
know if it was true or not but the cowboys claimed it was. It makes more
sense to me that she might have tried to ride a horse with the dress on and
the horse spooked from all that material flopping in the breeze, but that
was the way Ike told the story.

While working on the JA's, Ike got to be friends with Henry Rowden,
a cowboy who had been working there since 1907. More will be written
about Henry in future chapters.

Ike said there were lots of prairie dog holes out in the Texas Panhandle,
and that horses would step in them quite often. He recalled that the JA

ranch had a horse they called Mule. Ike said, "Mule was kind of a bronc and would pitch at tumbleweeds or about anything that moved." One time, Ike was riding him while chasing a steer, and Mule stepped in a prairie dog hole and fell down with Ike. Ike got on him and ran him back over it again, trying to teach him to look out for it, but the horse stepped in it and fell again. The boss running the wagon yelled, "Run him over it again!" Ike did it a third time and got the same result, so he finally gave up. Mule never learned. This story of yet another of Ike's many wild escapades never failed to make him laugh.

The cowboys had to create their own entertainment during the evenings at the bunk houses and around the chuck wagons. Other than their dancing, they would recite cowboy poetry, sing songs about their way of life, and shoot craps and gamble with one another.

Though Ike had been having fun working the JA ranch, he had gotten wind that out in Arizona they were paying a cowpuncher $50 a month. It was all Arizona Territory, no fences, and all free range. What really got his attention, though, was he heard you could rope all the cattle you could catch. The US government was paying $1 per head to the ranches for the beef, for any wild cattle that could be caught. Ike thought this would sure suit him better if he could rope more, so in March 1915, he left the JA Ranch, caught a train, and headed further west[1] (also see appendix 2).

FOUR

The Chiricahua Cattle Company and the Double Circles, 1915–1917

Marc 1915 found Ike en route to Fort Apache, Arizona, his destination. But the train had to make a stop and he had to change trains. He should have taken the train to Lordsburg, New Mexico, but by mistake he boarded the one headed to El Paso, Texas. As Ike related later, "I was a big ole twenty-two year old kid and had never been further than West Texas and didn't know my way around then." This statement certainly could not be said of his life hereafter.

PANCHO VILLA

The new train had to make a stop at Hachita, New Mexico. While at Hachita, Ike heard that the big Palomas outfit just south of the border in Old Mexico was paying $150 for two days' work to try to get back their cattle that Pancho Villa had been stealing. This was a ton of money for a very dangerous excursion. Ike, of course, thought it sounded interesting. Pancho Villa had been raiding the ranchers, killing people, and stealing their cattle and horses. Ranchers were desperately trying to get their stock back. During the 1910s, Pancho Villa became infamous for his spectacular success as a raider, robber, and murderer. His path of ruthlessness stretched from northern Mexico up across the border into Texas and New Mexico.

"The following year in March 1916 Villa kidnapped and killed eighteen Americans and launched a raid on Columbus, New Mexico, killing eighteen more Americans and burning the town. Villa lost around one hundred men due to the US Army presence. In retaliation for the raid, President Woodrow Wilson appointed General John J. Pershing to lead a

'Punitive Expedition' to capture or kill Pancho Villa. Ultimately the raid was unsuccessful, but the process of deploying troops and carrying out a large invasion of hostile territory helped prepare some of the US Army when the US declared war on Germany in April 1917."[1]

A cowboy that Ike befriended who had already been in Mexico searching for raided stock told Ike he could spend the night with him at his cabin. In the night, Ike heard a couple of little kids crying. The next morning Ike asked who those kids belonged to. His friend said that he came upon them the day after Pancho Villa had raided and killed their parents, and he felt sorry for them and brought them back with him. Ike had also heard of others who had been killed. Ike decided the money wasn't worth it and he'd better stick to his plan to get on to Arizona.

WORKING AT THE CHIRICAHUA'S

Ike then took the train on to Fort Apache, Arizona. The Fort Apache Indian Reservation was quite different—it was all open country at the time, and a lot more unsettled than the large ranches in West Texas that Ike was used to working.

Ike was at Fort Apache about ten to fifteen days searching for ranch work when a man by the name of John Osborne came into his hotel and asked if any of the cowboys there wanted to go to work for the Chiricahua Ranch (or the "Cherry Cows" as some old-timers called it, a corruption of "Chiricahua"). John worked for the Chiricahua Cattle Company, a huge cattle ranch that was incorporated in 1885 by eight ranchers at the north end of the Sulphur Springs Valley. The ranchers had pooled their assets in order to form one large ranch consisting of 1.6 million acres of grazing land and water rights, making it one of Arizona's largest cattle ranches. The ranch was in northern Cochise County and extended north into Graham County, and it was thirty-five miles wide and seventy-five miles long. In addition to their "owned" land, they also ran cattle on the Apache Reservation east of Globe, and it was here that John Osborne was hiring. They ran around 75,000 head of cattle at that location, depending on how many wild ones they could catch. They needed cowboys to bring wild cattle out of the mountains. All the other men were gambling and didn't pay much attention or show much interest, but Ike said, "I'll go." Ike figured this would be a great opportunity to do lots of roping and not get in trouble for it. Ike was hired and rode off with John.

This country was in the high White Mountains range, with tall pine trees and lots and lots of rocks, cliffs, gullies, and brush where wild cattle could run in and hide. It was quite unlike the wide-open ranges of West Texas. "It was a spread that embraced most of the San Carlos Indian Reservation and took three days for a man to ride across."[2] The terrain was more rugged, the brush was thicker, and there were many rocks. Twenty-some years prior, the area, just northeast of Globe, was where the famed Tonto Basin War, or Pleasant Valley War as referred to by some historians, had taken place between two feuding families, the Tewksburys and the Grahams.

This was far too rough of a country in which to pull a chuck wagon. Instead, a "pack outfit" was used, consisting of twelve to fifteen pack mules bearing all the kitchen pots, pans, food, and whatnot that would be needed to go up in the mountains and live for a period of time. The mules, and sometimes a few horses, carried the cowboys' bedrolls also. Ike recalled that the cow horses here were not as good as those in West Texas, but they could handle the rocky terrain a lot better. The horses had to have shoes put on them to handle the rocks. Each cowboy was responsible for shoeing his own string of horses. Here, each cowboy was assigned fifteen to twenty horses. Ike said that they would usually take five horses at a time and use them for about three or four weeks, then bring them back to the camp, turn them out for rest, and get five more fresh horses. Most of the work of catching the wild cattle was in the mountains, not the high plains. On the high plains the cattle were fairly gentle, but in the mountains, it was a different story. Those wild cattle were a real challenge to catch. They were smart. Sometimes they would run right back toward you and charge a horse. If this happened, they would sometimes kill a horse with their horns. Cowboys had to be really fast and on their guard to get out of the way. Cows would hide in the brush and watch you while you were looking for them. They were difficult to catch. The only way to get them was to rope them, and that was very difficult because of all the brush. When they were flushed out, a cowboy would have to rope fast before the cows would duck back into more brush. All this meant that Ike was doing a lot of roping, having fun, and not getting in trouble for doing it!

"Hard and fast" roping was the style practiced out in this country, meaning the rope was tied to the saddle horn, not dallied as is done in present times. There was no roping and tripping, as was done on the Matadors and JAs. The rough country didn't have room to lay a trip and drag the cattle in order to tie them. Heading and heeling, more than single roping, was the main way of catching cattle in this location. It was a very different way to handle cattle, but it was necessary because the cattle were extremely wild and ready for a fight if caught. Once a wild cow had been roped, the cowboy would snub it up to a tree by its horns and then leave it without food or water. Letting a wild cow wrestle the rope for a couple of days made its head sore and took some of the fight out of it. When the cowboy returned to get the cow, he would first tip the horns so that if the cow tried to hook the cowboy or his horse it wouldn't cause quite so much injury. Next he would untie the rope from the tree and then dally his rope around his saddle horn, keeping the line tight around the cow's horns to lead the cow down the mountain to the holding area. Ike said that for the first thirty minutes a cow might try to "get up in the saddle with you"—meaning that they would fight and charge your horse and try to jump up on it—but after that, they would generally lead like a puppy dog. Ike relayed, "It took sure enough good cowpunchers to rope and handle the cattle up there in those mountains."

The cattle would be herded down the mountains to a gathering area, wherever that might be in an open area down from the rugged terrain, and held together in a herd. There were no corrals or fences here, so three or four cowboys would have to keep them herded together and stay with them both night and day. The other cowboys would be out roping and catching some more to bring down the mountain to the holding place, one by one. When they had gathered a large number of wild cows, they would then drive them to the shipping points. After that, the process of catching more started all over again.

Stampedes occurred fairly regularly up in the mountains, as there were many more elements that could scare the cattle. Plus, they spooked easier than West Texas cattle. Anything from a storm with lightning and thunder to the sparks from a cowboy lighting a cigarette at night could spook a wild cow and start the whole herd on a stampede. Even the bawl of another cow could scare the others. Ike guessed the cattle must have had a way of communicating with one another with their bawlings, as it was only on some occasions that they would start a stampede. One sure learned a lot from and about wild cattle in those mountains. In a stampede, not too many cattle died from being trampled. Ike said, "You sure don't want to try to stop them during one. Just get out of their way and when they quit running, then try to gather them up again." Moviegoers might notice that this wisdom is entirely different from what the movies portray of cowboys trying to stop or herd cattle during a stampede. Ike said the real danger was for a man to get trampled, or they might run over a horse. That is why it was best to leave them alone until they were through running, then, the next morning, gather them all up again. In a lightning storm at night, he said that the lightning would be attracted to the wet cattle horns and it would jump from one set to another. It was quite a display! Because of all the rocks in the mountains, when stampedes occurred, they could sometimes smell the cows' hooves burning. Also because of the rocky terrain, a green horse didn't buck as much as when they were out in the open range.

Ike used to tell of putting "oxen shoes" on some of the better bulls that the ranchers wanted to preserve for breeding with the wild cows. This was done in order to protect their feet as much as possible from the rocks. Ike recalled one time shoeing about 135 bulls. They would put them in a chute, put a pipe under their belly to jack them up, and tie their feet together so they could work on them while they nailed on the shoes. They did not have portable chutes back then to bring to where they were working the cattle, so they had to build their own makeshift chutes from the timber at hand. Even if they would have had them, they would have been of no use as there would not have been a way to transport them through the rough terrain where they were working. He said they "quicked" them a lot—bruising their hooves when nails aren't driven in properly to attach them to the hoof—but turpentine was put on their feet to help them heal. They would then release the bulls back in the mountains to breed with the cows. Ike said these shoes would eventually be worn off, but he had run across twenty-five or thirty bulls that still had their shoes on after six months.

Lightning storms were frequent and dangerous up in the tall pine country, as a strike could hit the tops of the trees and bring them down. Ike recalled one heavy rainstorm when he had been galloping his horse trying to get back to camp. He happened to pull his horse up for a brief second so his horse could get his wind. No sooner had he stopped when about a hundred feet in front of him lightning hit a huge pine and knocked it down right in his path. Ike said it was brought down with such force that about half of the tree was stuck in the ground like a spear. He would have been killed if he had kept on going and hadn't stopped when he did.

Ike tried to go to any roping contests that were held at any of the close mountain towns within a ride of a day or two. Because of Ike's good roping skills, his boss, John Osborne, would often pay Ike's entry fees for him and send him off on horseback. John always called Ike "Little Boy" because of his stature.

Ike never had any trouble with the Apaches, but he said he came upon a lot of wagons, wheels, and other evidence where people had been attacked and killed by them. The Mormons had moved into Arizona from the North some years prior and the Apaches had killed many of them. Ike had arrived in this area several years after most of these occurrences, but he heard lots of stories from the older men about these attacks.

DOUBLE CIRCLES

Sometime in the year 1916 Ike found work for a neighboring ranch in the same vicinity, the Double Circles. "The Double Circles was on Eagle Creek, with headquarters at Clifton, near the New Mexico line. The ranch included range land in the Mogollon Mountains—rough country."[3]

That is where Ike saw one of the wildest events of cow work that he had ever witnessed. A cowboy, Pete Farley, had come back to get a white stag that had been tied to a tree for a couple of days. The stag was about six or seven years old. The stag's horns had already been tipped. When the cowboy put his rope around the stag's horns and secured the other end to his saddle, he then cut the rope that had tied it to the tree. Once the wild steer was released, it jumped up into Pete's saddle and started fighting with him. His horse ran about 150 yards trying to get away from the wild steer while up above the cowboy was trying to fight off its attacks. Finally, Pete managed to knock the raging animal down from on top of him and his horse and get it under control. Years later, when reminiscing about this event, Ike said he doubted that any of the rodeo cowboys he had encountered in later years could have handled a wild cow on attack like Pete did that day. It took a real cowboy who knew how to handle wild cattle to come out alive from an episode like that.

Three cowboys from the Matadors and JAs whom Ike had worked with previously, Tom Blasingame, Henry Rowden, and one other unidentified, came out to Arizona to get a job. Tom Wilson, who was running the Double Circles then, told them he was "full up" and couldn't use them. Ike talked to Wilson and said, "These men are sure enough cowboys and you need to hire them." Tom changed his mind then and put them to work breaking horses.

During Christmas time in 1916, the Double Circle Ranch held a "burro" team roping for entertainment. All participating cowboys rode burros. Ike teamed with Pete Farley. There is no record of whether they won.

Tom Blasingame remembered the time he spent at the Double Circles:

> It was a monster outfit. They didn't know how big it was. We'd make big drives and throw the cattle together and brand and cut what we wanted to ship out. They had a big holding pasture in the center of the range where we'd put 'em, then we'd turn the others loose and brand 'em. We had plenty of wood in that country; so, it was easy to make a good fire.
>
> We lived outside all the time. We had our bedrolls rollup in a tarp. If it was raining, we'd just cover up with our tarps and sit there. We'd bathe in the river. It was pretty cold sometimes. We lived on beef and pinto beans. The meat kept fine outdoors. It was a lot better than this Frigidaire meat, you bet. Down on the desert outfits, they made lots of jerky. I'd eat it with biscuits if they was good, or I'd just eat it straight. You didn't have many good bread cooks out in the camp. In the wintertime, we'd have them steaks for breakfast, and gravy. It was a pack outfit, so you didn't get eggs or anything like that. It had to be stuff you could pack, but I never got tired of eating the same thing all the time.
>
> At the Circles, we'd go to town on the Fourth of July and Christmas. Most of the cowboys would get drunk, but I never did take to that whiskey. Drinkers, they're pretty disgustin' when they get down and waller on the ground, mumblin' and stumblin' and vomitin.' Course, I'd go to the saloons. There was music going all the time. Them dancin' girls would come out there onstage. You ever heard a song called Mexicali Rose? Well, I saw her. She was a beauty, all right, a tall, slim brunette. She sure could sing.
>
> On Christmas, we'd hurry back to the ranch because that's when they'd have them big dances. People would come from a hundred miles on horseback; women, children, and all. They'd pack their good clothes on little mules. They'd stay around a week and dance all night

and sleep in the daytime. We'd lay around and run horse races, and a lot of 'em would play poker and kill time till night when they'd go to dancin' again. Don't ever think that people who lived way out like that couldn't dance. Man, they could dance, waltz, one-step, square dance, you bet. Even them little kids could square dance. That was the prettiest thing to watch.[4]

The only medicine available if someone got sick was Epsom salts. It could be as much as forty-five miles to the nearest town to a doctor. If you did break a bone or got hurt, you would just have to saddle up and ride to town or else just try to endure it. Ike said there was an old Indian chief who would usually doctor the cowboys the best he could. But for the most part, hardly anyone ever caught colds or was sick. It's pretty amazing to think that sleeping out in the mountains in those kinds of elements would not be a problem! Also amazing was that Ike and most of the other hands weren't hurt seriously, considering the type of work they did every day. This is evidence they all were very experienced cowboys.

There was no dentist out on the ranch, either. Ike told a story about a bad toothache that struck another "cowboy character" he was friends with— Breezy Cox—while they were together way up in the Arizona mountains and a good long ride to any town. Breezy was one of the best cowboys Ike had ever worked with and was a good roper. They both had been drinking, Breezy presumably because of the pain, and Ike perhaps just for "moral support." Well, Breezy asked Ike to take some fencing pliers and pull the tooth for him. Ike wanted to make sure he got the right tooth so Breezy showed him which one it was. Ike told Breezy to lie down on the ground and he would pull it. Ike got on top of him and put his knees on Breezy's shoulders and pulled it. After the ordeal, Breezy jumped up and told Ike that he had pulled the wrong tooth! Ike told him to lie back down and he would pull the correct one, which he did! You never know what kind of goings-on to expect from a cowboy like Breezy, who just happened to be the brother-in-law of Arizona steer roper Carl Arnold.

Another Arizona cowboy, Pecos Higgins—a bronc rider who had worked many of the same locations as Ike, also in the White Mountains, on the Chiricahuas, Double Circles, Flying Hs and the Flying Bs, and about everywhere in Arizona—wrote one of Ike's favorite poems. Ike had always felt it fit him. He would recite this poem many years later, in a 1968 radio interview at Pendleton, Oregon, and again in 1969, in a four-hour taped interview with Charles Townsend for Texas Tech University. It typifies the cowboy's life in that era:

Hell on the Mountainside
by Pecos Higgins

It was away out on the Mountains, among the lonesome pine
Where the quakin' ash grows thick as hell
And so does the wild grapevine
Where you hunt your saddle horses
In canyon, vail, and dell
And you put out your eyes
A lookin' for tracks
And your ears a listenin' for a bell.

Cowpunchin' was once a pleasure
When there was lots of good old hands
And herds of good cow ponies
That damn nigh knew the brands
But today they got us bested
The cows they understand
For they may head out for the bushes
Or some awful broken land.

Them days when the roundup was over
It was off to town we'd go
We'd have a drink of whiskey
Maybe a dozen or so
The bartender he would greet us
And the girls would call us in
But them good ole days have come and gone
They're classed now as sin.

This world has made many changes
Since I came on this soil
There's nothing but hardships
Lonesome trials and toil
Cows, they've got us bested
Out where the woodvine twine
Not many cowboys left
That can neck one to a pine.

Chapter 4

These chaps around the cities
That wear the cowboy's clothes
Would be wearin' a g-string
If they knew a puncher's woes
If it was up to them to gather stock
In the canyon, briar, and leaf
We'd all be out of luck
And damn sure out of beef.

Last night as I lay in my soogins
They were neither soft nor warm
They've never felt the presence
Of a Maiden's lovely form
Away up in the big old pine tree
Was a hootin' of an owl
And deep down in the canyon
Was a lonesome lobo's howl.

This time last year I was all dressed up
I was drunk as I could be
Right among the pretty gals
With all the sights to see
We rode the Spanish ponies
And roped ole Billy the Kid
We popped a maiden's coat tails
Just as soon as the sun was hid.

But today, I'm all by my lonesome
Out in a little tent
Just another year has come and gone
And awfully, badly, spent
But the cards, they may break in the next one
That's what I think
I'll have me a pretty gal
And lots of booze to drink.

If not, I'll go down to Old Mexico
Where there's lot of good mescal
I may even join the Mormons
Or marry a Mexican gal.
So farewell you city slickers
With your loathsome sober lives
For I'll die out in the jungles
A lonely but contented life.

At camp one evening high in the mountains, the cowboys were playing pitch when a man from headquarters, which was fifty miles away, rode in on horseback. He had a very important letter from the US government to be delivered to Ike Rude. It had arrived at headquarters, where it sat for two weeks as they were trying to locate in what part of the mountains the cowboys might be found. It said Ike had been drafted, for the Great War had started (later referred to as World War I), and he was to report immediately. By this time the letter was six months old, as it had first been sent to his boyhood town of Mangum, Oklahoma. All his parents knew was that he was somewhere in the White Mountains of Arizona. From there, the US government had somehow found out what cattle outfit he was working for, and that is how they tracked him down. Ike was scared to death. He figured he was now in a heap of trouble since the notice was so long getting to him, so he immediately saddled a horse and headed down the mountains to Bisbee, Arizona, to contact the US Army and to catch a train. When Ike got to Bisbee, he contacted US officials to explain why he was only now reporting in, due to where he had been and why he had just then received the notice. They told him to just wait. The regiment he was supposed to be in had already shipped to San Antonio, Texas. They would call him on the next round of draft now that they knew how to reach him. So Ike headed back, a hundred fifty miles, on horseback, to the Double Circles (also see appendix 2).[5]

FIVE

The Great War, 1918–1919

The Great War started July 28, 1914, but the United States did not start sending troops until 1917 and not in large numbers until mid-1918. It is now referred to as World War I, but at the time it started, there had never been a world war before.

In March 1918, Ike got his second draft notice. He caught a train home to see his parents for a few days. He thought this would be the last time he would ever see them again. Therefore, he'd better make a stop in Mangum, Oklahoma, before he left for the war.

He was then sent by train to San Antonio, Texas, for three weeks of training. After the training, he was sent to Brooklyn, New York, and then to France with the 90th Division, made up of drafted Texans and Oklahomans that became known as the "Fighting Ninetieth," or the "Tough Ombres" because of their TO (Texas/Oklahoma) symbol on their uniform shoulder patches. The ship first took him to England for seventy-three days, then on to France, and then Germany.

"Ike was with the 315th Mobile Veterinary Section which was attached to the 357th Infantry. His job was to bring injured horses back from the front lines. Ike made the battle of St. Mihiel and the Meuse-Argonne push in the fall of 1918, some of the roughest fighting in history. The 90th Division lost more men than any other American drafted division. Ike said no more than four or five originals of a lot of the companies survived."[1]

"Horses and mules provided the primary source of power for the Great War. Over 8 million horses and mules served in World War I; over 1.3 million came from the United States. Some were mustangs from the US Great Plains states and Canadian provinces and were half wild. Between 1914 and 1917, 1,000 horses per day from North America were sent across the Atlantic. The lack of space for horses and mules on transport ships directly affected the number of horses and mules (and trucks) accessible to the AEF upon landing in France.

"Cavalry, artillery, services of supply, and ambulances all used horses and mules. For example, the four-ton French 75mm gun and carriage required a team of six horses or mules to pull it. After January 1918, US Army procurement officers in Europe found horses and mules in short supply and expensive and most had already been rejected by the French army. The average service life of a horse or mule in World War I was ten days. A large number of handlers and trainers of horses and muleteers in the AEF were African American."[2]

The military used horses and mules mainly for logistical support; they were better than mechanized vehicles at traveling through deep mud and over rough terrain. Horses and mules were used for carrying messengers as well as for pulling artillery, ambulances, and supply wagons. The presence of horses and mules often increased morale among the soldiers at the front, but the animals contributed to disease and poor sanitation in camps, caused by their manure and carcasses. The value of horses and mules and the increasing difficulty of replacing them were such that by 1917, some troops were told that the loss of a horse or mule was of greater tactical concern than the loss of a human soldier. Ultimately, the blockade of Germany prevented the Central Powers from importing horses and mules to replace those lost, which contributed to Germany's defeat. Conditions were severe for horses and mules at the front; they were killed by artillery fire, suffered from skin disorders, and were injured by poison gas. Hundreds of thousands of horses and mules died, and many more were treated at veterinary hospitals and sent back to the front. Several memorials have been erected to commemorate the horses and mules that died in the Great War.

Ike's job was to bring injured horses and mules, at least those that could be saved, back from the front lines. The ones who were still alive, but could not be saved, were to be shot and killed. Ike was sent to the front lines to do this as the battles were being fought. He was sent behind the machine guns and ahead of the infantry. It was an extremely dangerous and a potentially deadly situation.

The Meuse-Argonne was a major part of the final offense for World War I. It was fought from September 26, 1918, to November 11, 1918, forty-seven days. It was the largest in US history, involving 1.2 million American soldiers, and it was the second-deadliest battle in US history. The US mortality rate was worsened by the inexperience of many of the troops and the widespread onset of the global influenza outbreak called the "Spanish flu."

On November 11, 1918, World War I ended. Ike was ordered to remain in Germany, where he served eight months of occupation duty.

While in Germany, Ike attended a horse show and met two Oklahoma cowboys who were also serving there: Fred Lowry, a top cowboy from

Ike Rude at Bern Castle, Germany, during World War I, 1918.

Lenapah, Oklahoma, who had won the famed steer roping at Cheyenne, Wyoming, in 1916, just two years prior, and Lewis Jones, another top roper of whom Ike often said, many years later, was the best goat roper he had ever known. The trio decided to put on a goat roping as a special show for the Germans. Jones told Ike that he had seen a trailer that you could pull behind a car and put a horse in it. It could go fifteen miles per hour! Race horses were being transported in England in this manner.

After the German occupation, Ike was sent home to the United States, and on June 20, 1919, at El Paso, Texas, he received his discharge papers.

Once discharged from the army, Ike went home to Mangum for a short spell. He then heard of a rodeo being held in Oklahoma City, a hundred fifty miles away. Ike saddled one of his dad's horses and rode to Oklahoma City to rope in his first "professional" rodeo. There was no official organization of rodeos at this time, but Oklahoma City had attracted most of the cowboys that had been roping as their main profession, and it was offering some higher purses. He was scared to death when it came time for him to rope and it was raining hard. He didn't win anything.

By this time, his dad, Sam Rude, had sold all his cattle and had been elected chief of police of Mangum, a job he held until his death in 1938.

Ike with his horses Blue Darter and Ol' Paint, 1919. Ike Rude in the Saddle House, unknown photographer, undated, photographic postcard. Willard H. Porter Rodeo Collection, Dickinson Research Center, National Cowboy and Western Heritage Museum. 2001.049.

Ike's uncle, Joe Rude, provided Ike a job farming his fifty acres of wheat. The twenty-five-year-old veteran tried his hand at a new career, but found out, right quick, that farming was not in his DNA.

The next spring, his father gave him a big gray horse that he had used to drive and cut out hogs, just like cattle is cut from the herd. He was always just called "the hog horse," but he was of Peter McCue breeding. Peter McCue was a legendary sire that had stood at stud at Cheyenne, Oklahoma, in 1910. After his father gave him the horse, Ike renamed him "Blue Darter." The horse took to working cattle in a remarkable way with Ike training and roping on him. In all likelihood, Darter's early job of cutting hogs is what made him into the horse he was to become. Hogs are quicker than cattle. Blue Darter would become the first of many horses that was outstanding in Ike's future as an owner and trainer of famous roping horses. Now that Ike had "transportation," it was time to get back to something he enjoyed more than farming, so he headed back to the JA Ranch, eighty miles west of Mangum, to see if he could work there again (also see appendix 2).

SIX

Back to the JAs, 1920–1921

By 1920, Ike was once again working for the JA Ranch in West Texas, where he found himself among a few familiar faces. One was Tom Blasingame, who had worked alongside Ike at the Double Circles in Arizona. Tom had worked for the JAs as early as 1916, and was back again. The two formed a fast friendship that lasted the remainder of their lives.

Henry Rowden, who had also previously worked with Ike, but over at the Matador Ranch, was now at the JAs, too. Henry liked the ladies, and he was constantly calling the telephone switchboard at Silverton, Texas, just to talk to the female operators. Mrs. Adair, the owner of the JAs, would come from England at least once a year to check on things. When she came, she would bring a good many of her maids with her, all young women. Henry especially liked this time at the ranch, and was constantly hanging around the "big house," which is what the cowboys called the main house where the boss lady and her maids stayed during their visits to the ranch. This really aggravated the general manager, J. W. Kent, as Henry wasn't tending to his work during this time. J. W. told Ike that he was going to break Henry of this habit, so the next time Mrs. Adair came with her entourage, Henry was ordered to take all the maids for a horseback ride. They were all from England and had never been on a horse before. Henry was told to go catch and saddle the gentlest horses. He had to help each one of the ladies onto her horse, and, as he told Ike later, "It was like lifting a sack of potatoes." It must have been quite the ordeal, for when Henry finally got back from his "day's work" of taking the maids for their first horseback ride, he said he never wanted to hang around the big house again! All the men sure got a kick out of this.

One weekend when the cowboys were taking it easy lounging around the JA headquarters, Ike apparently was looking for some excitement, and of course excitement to him meant something he could rope! "He looked out across the pasture and spotted an old buffalo grazing alone that had been run off from the herd. At that time ninety to one hundred head of wild buffalo still roamed on the JA ranch. The younger bulls would run the older bulls off from the herd. Ike tells his bunkhouse partner, let's go rope him. His partner tells him that neither one of the horses they were riding had been trained yet to be roped from, as they were only recently broke to ride. Ike's reply was that they have to learn some time. Before his partner could get his horse saddled, Ike was already on his horse and taking out after the buffalo. The first loop he threw caught the buffalo and when it did, Ike and the horse went flying in the air and the rope broke. When they landed, Ike got up and told his partner to lend him his rope, as he was going to try it again. Well, his partner thought this was getting a little too wild for him—if Ike wanted to kill himself he didn't want to be part of it. So he decided to go back to the bunkhouse. He said along about mid-afternoon Ike came back. He asked Ike how it went . . . Ike's reply was, "I lost another rope."[1] Long-time JA manager Jack Moreman, in a video interview nearly a hundred years later, shared this story about Ike that was still told around the ranch. Ike's partner said the rope breaking was probably the only thing that saved Ike's life!

> Ike achieved a certain reputation for fearlessness. On the sandy banks of the Red River in north Texas in 1921, older waddies tipped their sweat-stained Stetsons to the nerviest young guy in the beef-on-the-hoof business.
>
> Five-hundred head of yearling steers had been driven to the south bank of the "Big Red." They were, recalled Ike, to be crossed immediately. But the river was on a rampage of swift-moving, muddy slush. Waves humped up in the middle like dirty ocean surf and, staring at them, cranky and more than a little horrified, a half dozen wranglers wished they had never seen a cow.
>
> Ike and a buddy, Henry Rowden, took the two points. They jumped the 600- pound steers off into the swirling, cocoa-colored water. The steers bawled and pawed the curling swells that slopped over them. Ike and Rowden kept them swimming with curses, yells, songs and threats. In 30 minutes, exhausted and half drowned, the entire herd was drying off on the north bank.

"I took my leggin's off," Ike told me, "and tied 'em to my saddle. If I lost my horse I wanted to be able to swim. Some of the old boys that followed us up said it was the wildest event they ever laid eyes on. I guess it was, too. We were under the river more than on top. You know, you can tell if an old boy's done any horse swimming by the way he goes about it. The easiest way is to slip out of the saddle, get on your horse's hip and grab him by the tail."[2]

Ike had roped so much by this time that he was one of the privileged few who were called on to rope the calves and drag them to the fires at branding time. It was usually the straw boss who did this job. One roper on a good horse could keep two or three teams of flankers busy. Flankers were the cowboys on foot who would throw and hold the calves for the branding, castration, and, later, vaccination operations. There were no chutes to run the cattle into during those years.

Ike was twenty-six years old, having already roped more cattle than some cowboys get to in a lifetime. Ranch general manager J. W. Kent was very impressed with Ike's roping ability, and would become the turning point in Ike's dream of becoming the best roper in the world. In the spring of 1921, Kent bet $500 with the boss of the neighboring RO Ranch that Ike could beat the best roper among the cowboys that worked on the RO Ranch in goat roping, then a popular sport in Texas. Of all the things Ike had roped up to then, not too many of them had been goats. But Ike wasn't going to admit there wasn't anything he couldn't rope better than anybody. So he started practicing and was doing quite well—so well that once his ability became known, the bet got called off. Ike decided not to let the time be wasted that he had put into roping goats, so he entered some contests. J. W. would let Ike off work to go to neighboring towns to enter the local goat ropings. Always, Ike would ride his horse Blue Darter to and from the ropings. In a matter of weeks, he had won about $2,000. This sure beat cowpuncher wages! By then Ike was being paid $75 a month working for the JA Ranch.

Goat ropings and steer ropings were all that were held in that area at that time. Calf roping did not come onto the scene until very shortly afterward, but when it did, it replaced goat ropings. Ike roped goats in both Texas and Oklahoma at this time: Shamrock, McLean, Wellington, Clarendon, Claude, and Canadian, Texas, and Hollis, Mangum, Erick, and

Sayre, Oklahoma. Ike won his first big steer roping in 1921 at Cheyenne, Oklahoma. Other winnings in steer roping were at Sayre, Erick, and Hollis, Oklahoma.

In April 1921, Mrs. Cornelia Adair came to her ranch from England for one last time. It was her eighty-fourth birthday and she wanted a group picture of herself with all of "her boys." The cowboys all dressed in their finest for the occasion. Under the picture was captioned, "No queen ever had more loyal subjects than the women who controlled large ranching enterprises." After returning to England, Mrs. Adair passed away on September 22, 1921. Shortly after the photo was taken, Ike decided it was time to quit his cow punching job, hit the road, and pursue his dream (also see appendix 2).[3]

Mrs. Cornelia Adair and the JA Boys, a portrait taken on the occasion of her eighty-fourth birthday, April 1921. Ike is third from the left, seated.

SEVEN

Blue Darter, 1921–1933

ke and his horse Blue Darter lost no time in getting to the next steer, goat, or calf roping, whether on horseback or by train. If he had to take a train, the only mode of transporting a horse at the time, Ike would bed down with Darter in the stock car in order to feed and water him. He then heard of a goat and calf roping at Iowa Park, Texas, organized by Tom Burnett, owner of the 6666 Ranch. Calf roping was just catching on. Ike saddled Blue Darter with a bedroll and the one rope he had, and headed to it, a hundred thirty miles to Iowa Park from the Salt Fork River, where he was at the time. (Imagine riding your roping horse that far, then competing on him!) Arriving the night before the roping, Ike bedded down in the OK Wagon Yard. Next morning, by the time he found the roping grounds at the 6666, the event had already started. Ike found Tom Burnett and told him he sure would like to enter if it wasn't too late. Tom told Ike that it was pretty stiff competition, that there had already been some goats tied in eleven seconds in the goat roping. That didn't sway Ike, so Tom let him enter late.

Ike tied his first goat in ten seconds to win the round. Ike won all three go-rounds in the goat roping. Then the calf roping was next. One of the main attractions of having ropings was so people could wager. Not too many bet on a guy that only stood 5'6" (with his boots on) and weighed 125 pounds. The calves were large and rank, right off the 6666 Ranch.

The calves were tough and 24 seconds was in the lead. Just as Tom Burnett was commenting he'd like to have seen a calf tied in twenty, but figured there was no shot—Ike wiped one out in twenty seconds flat—to win the go-round with a four second cushion. Winning the second go-round, he had 'em by the handle going to the third and last calf. Just as he laced it on him, that calf stumbled and turned a

47

flip and Ike came up with a "seldom" empty loop. Riding back to the chutes, they asked, "How come you didn't take another loop?" With that grin that became one of the best known throughout the west in the next half century, Ike said, "Heck, I didn't know you could use another loop." Foghorn Clancy was announcing and he made the most of it and Ike made a lot of friends that day.[1]

The famed George Weir from New Mexico was also roping there. George was one of the very best veteran ropers at the time. After Ike's astonishing win, beating all the "who's who" of roping, George befriended Ike and asked him to go back to Whizbang, Oklahoma, with him. The first roping Weir took him to at Whizbang, Ike won it. Ike said, "We sure had fun. The town was booming and somebody got shot nearly every night." Whizbang had a history of being a wild and lawless place. It is now a ghost town.

While at Whizbang, Ike met Barton Carter, a cowboy from Pawhuska, Oklahoma, where Ike went next after the roping in Whizbang. Ike won first in Pawhuska, too, and he and Barton became fast friends, with Barton asking Ike to come stay with him at his ranch. Ike's "stay" turned into around ten years. The two bachelors had a grand time going to rodeos and carousing around in Barton's car. Automobiles were becoming popular about this time. Ike didn't know how to drive, and hadn't owned one yet. When they weren't practicing roping, the two liked to tour the country and drive around to the neighboring ranches and check on their roping buddies and their competition. Everett Shaw used to complain that they never came down to Stonewall, Oklahoma, to see him. They told him that he had too much work to do what with putting up hay on his small ranch, and not enough slack time to rope and have fun!

Around 1921, C. B. Irwin hired Ike to rope at his rodeos. C. B. was one of the earliest stock contractors that had enough livestock of his own to produce rodeos. He was the stock contractor and manager for years of the "Daddy of 'em All," the Cheyenne Frontier Days in Cheyenne, Wyoming. Ike traveled with this rodeo production for a time. King Merritt was also working for C. B. as a roper, and he became another of Ike's lifelong friends. They both were born in 1894, had both worked at the Matador and JA ranches in Texas, though not at the same time, and also served in World War I.

Ike (*left*) and King Merritt, 1925. "Both were 31 years old. They were pals and a couple of the best steer ropers to ever swing a loop," said Willard Porter in his article "A Visit with Ike Rude," in *The Quarter Horse Journal,* November 1973.

In the year 1922, goat roping was becoming scarce and being replaced by calf roping, but before it was completely phased out, Ike roped goats at Copan, Oklahoma. That year, he roped calves at Turley, Broken Arrow, Bristow, Coweta, Pawhuska, and Bigheart, Oklahoma; Denver and Limon, Colorado; and North Platte, Nebraska, to name a few. In 1922, Madison Square Garden in New York City held its first rodeo. Ike and Blue Darter boarded the train and attended. This was to be the first of Ike's twenty-six years in a row (apart from 1934, when he went to London, England) to compete in the Garden's rodeo. He won third in the calf roping. Lee Robinson won first, with Ben Johnson Sr. taking second. That same year, when a matched roping between Ben Johnson Sr. (father of the rodeo star and actor Ben "Son" Johnson Jr.) and Ike was held at Shidler, Oklahoma, Ike came out the winner. In 1921 and 1922 he won seven Texas goat ropings and five in Oklahoma, plus one at Roswell, New Mexico, on Christmas Day, and another at Denver, Colorado.

FIRST HORSE TRAILER

It was during 1922 that Ike told Barton what he had learned about horse trailers while he was in Germany. Barton thought that sounded like a great idea, so the two decided to build one. Well, I'm sure Barton had to have been a much better carpenter than Ike, as Ike never could hit a nail on its head. They got it built and ready for a test run. Barton told Ike to go get Darter and load him in it to see if this contraption worked. Ike did have the good judgement to suggest they leave Darter out of it and just test it first without a horse. They did just that. All went well until something happened at the first sharp curve they came to, when the trailer came loose from the hitch and tore itself apart. Ike decided that the idea might not have been so good and he didn't want to chance losing his good roping horse, so he would just continue to catch a train or ride his horse to get to the rodeos like he had been doing. However, Barton still thought it was a good idea, so he rebuilt the trailer after Ike took off to some rodeos. The second year of the Madison Square Garden rodeo, 1923, Barton hauled his horse there in it. It was the "talk of the cowboys" that year. A guy by the name of Hale looked at it and had the idea to mass-produce it, thus beginning Hale Trailer Sales, the first company believed to mass-produce horse trailers for sale to the public. It is not officially known if Ike and Barton built the first horse trailer in the United States, as others returning to the United States from the war could have had the same idea. But it is documented as fact that this was the first—and they *believed* it to be the first—horse trailer Ike and Barton Carter had ever seen in all of their travels around the United States since the war.

Blue Darter was proving himself in a big way at steer roping as well as goat and calf roping, and Ike was winning consistently. During this era, in conjunction with the ropings, there were a lot of matched horse races. Betting was hugely popular for both the horse races and the roping events. Ike would often put Blue Darter in the races, and he was winning a lot of money for Ike in this also!

Right up there with roping and good horses, Ike always loved to gamble. For the next twenty-plus years, winning money became no problem for Ike, either by roping or shooting craps. Money never meant much to Ike. His view of it was that to have money just kept a person tied down to too many things. This was the reason he never thought about saving to buy a ranch anywhere. He knew so many cowboys who had to go home to take care of their cattle and other interests instead of going to the next rodeo. Ike wanted to be "footloose and fancy free," so to speak, and to be available to go rope at every rodeo or roping he could get to. Also, Ike was never in one place long enough to put money in a bank, as access was local. To his way of thinking, having a lot of money was a real hassle to have to carry around all of the time. So he would sometimes send some money home to his mother and sisters for their use. And when other cowboys were down on their luck, Ike would often pay their entry fees and give them a loan. The favor was often returned to Ike when he was in the same circumstances. Cowboys were, and still are, a close-knit group of people. They always help one another.

Ike also liked his whiskey and was most always a happy person. Even when he drank, people enjoyed being around him and listening to his wild cowboy stories and his colorful way of talking. He loved life and loved roping and had fun doing both, but when he roped, he was all business. He was a character, true to the old-time cowboy image.

While living at Pawhuska, Ike worked some on the Chapman-Barnard Ranch in his off-time from rodeoing. He also became fast friends with Ben Johnson Sr., who ran the ranch, as well as with Fred Lowry and Chock

Dyer, two other top ropers who lived nearby. The vicinity around Pawhuska was home to a good many of the nation's top steer ropers at that time, and still is an area that produces many top cowboys and cowgirls to this day in various rodeo events.

WILL ROGERS

Will Rogers was also at that first Madison Square Garden rodeo, working for the Ziegfeld Follies. He came over to the rodeo to perform an exhibition in calf roping and needed a horse to ride. After observing all the roping horses at work, he thought the best one was a big gray horse that Ike Rude was roping on. He asked Ike if he could borrow Blue Darter to rope on, and Ike let him. After the exhibition, Will offered Ike $1,000 for the horse but Ike turned the offer down. The spring of 1923, while Ike was roping at the Houston, Texas, rodeo, Will sent a telegram to Ike, this time offering $1,500. This was quite a remarkable price for a horse back in 1923! Ike replied via telegram with one word: "No." Will sent him another telegram that said, "Just price the horse." Ike's reply was that he was not for sale. Will sent him another telegram that said, "You are a damn fool for not pricing him." There is no telling what Will might have paid for the horse. Will was making a lot of money by then, both in the movies as well as at all of his engagements as a comedian, philosopher, and trick roper. Ike would recall decades later that he felt Will would have paid almost any price for Darter. "But I've never been sorry. That horse took me places I couldn't have gone without him," Ike said.

Will and Ike became close friends from then on. Whenever their paths would cross, Will would borrow Blue Darter to rope on for several performances. In the Will Roger's Memorial at Claremore, Oklahoma, there are several pictures displayed of Will roping off Blue Darter. During the 1920s and 1930s between rodeos, Ike would often hang out at the ranch owned by Will's nephew, Herb McSpadden, in Oologah, Oklahoma. Herb was actually living in the house in which Will had been born. Herb's son, Clem McSpadden, would become a state senator and prominent rodeo announcer. Will would often be at the ranch in between his performances.

The ranch wasn't the only place one might find Will and Ike together. Will would often go over to Arkansas City, Kansas, to watch Ike rope. These ropings were held there sometime from 1923 to 1930.

On one occasion, while Will and Ike were both in between engagements and staying at Oologah, they decided to have a matched goat roping at Wynona, Oklahoma, a little town a few minutes south of Pawhuska. Rumor has it they both put up $20. Of course, that was considerably more money back then. According to a report from Joe Snively, a top hand in steer roping who heard about it from his father, Jim Snively, a top calf and steer roper from 1929 through the 1950s, Ike and Will didn't have any chutes to put the goats in. They decided that they each would hold the goats for the other one and then release them when the other one was ready to chase and rope them. Will went first while Ike held the goat, and Will missed. Ike went to get his horse because it was his turn to rope next. He found Will's horse being loaded into its trailer. When Ike asked, "Aren't you going to hold my goat for me so I can rope?" Will stated he could see that he might be holding goats for Ike all day, as Ike wasn't going to miss. And since he, Will, had already missed his first goat, he would just concede to Ike. I'm

The unveiling of Shrine of the Sun at Colorado Springs, Colorado, in 1937, to honor Will Rogers after his death. Bob Crosby, All-Around Champion cowboy at Cheyenne Frontier Days and the Pendleton Round-Up in 1925, 1927, and 1928, is at the far left with rope in hand; Ike is second from the right, in khaki pants, arms folded.

pretty sure Ike must have been very disappointed, as, knowing him, he was just planning on several hours of roping and now he wouldn't get to!

After the death of Will and Wiley Post in a 1935 plane crash, a monument was erected in Colorado Springs, Colorado, in Will's honor, the Shrine of the Sun. In 1937, Ike attended the grand opening of the shrine to pay tribute to his friend.

By 1920, rodeos were drawing huge audiences, especially back east.

Ike's big gray horse, Blue Darter, was getting better all the time. Like most of the horses Ike eventually owned, Old Darter was so big that Ike had to jump to get his foot in the stirrup. In 1923, Ike, aboard Blue Darter, roped at his first Cheyenne "Daddy of 'em All" rodeo Frontier Days, where he won second place in the calf roping. First place went to Ike's friend George Cline, a roper from Arizona whom Ike had allowed to use his horse in the roping! After that trip to Cheyenne, Ike would rope there for the next forty-plus years. He always said, "I would go to Cheyenne just to hear the band play." This quote from Ike would be used in many articles and book chapters over the years. Cheyenne was always Ike's favorite rodeo. Cheyenne would also be the very last rodeo Ike would rope in, some forty-eight years later.

Also in 1923 he roped calves at Bartlesville and Dewey, Oklahoma; Henrietta, Texas; Denver, Colorado; and Yankee Stadium, New York, winning second there. Steer roper Bob Crosby won first. Ike steer roped at Salina, Kansas, at the last steer roping that was ever held there.

When Ike set out to rodeo, he meant business. He made it to all the major ones he could get to. Cowboys were huge celebrities then, especially on the East Coast, as people back east still believed myths and wild tales they had heard about cowboys and Indians in the West (some true and some not so true). The rodeos were a big draw, as entertainment was scarce then. The Humane Society added to the notoriety by constantly interfering with most of the timed and judged events, as they thought they were too cruel to animals. This is a concern to this day, leading many states to outlaw steer roping, or steer tripping as it is called today.

At Madison Square Garden, many celebrities would attend the rodeo and mingle with the cowboys afterward. Ike met Babe Ruth and Lou Gehrig. They gave him tickets to their baseball game. When Ike roped at

that we were humans just like them, they turned out to be a real nice bunch of people and did a wonderful business with us.

I have always felt that had we carried rain insurance from the start, or had waited thirty days to start the show; it would have been a huge financial success, as the people really like the show. I never quite figured out why the Humane Society was so rough on us. We fed our stock good and sure didn't abuse them intentionally. Every day while we were there, we would see little thin, sore footed dray horses being worked on trash routes and etc.

With the shows finished, we were ready to start back West, except for just one thing. The head honcho of the Knights of Columbus in Denver had to okay the release of the money to move the train. He had gone to the mountains on a fishing trip! There we all sat in Brooklyn for three days while they looked this guy up. During the waiting period, the Indians got to circulating around out in the residential district. When the people found out the Indians wouldn't scalp them, they started giving them old clothing, especially hats. It wasn't unusual to see a big buck coming down Flatbush Avenue wearing some lady's Easter Bonnet of a few years back, maybe being followed by "a little fat squaw" decked out in some gentleman's hard shelled caddy hat. It was a scream! We sold a few of our bareback horses to some Italians to make coal wagon horses out of. The last I saw of a big old bay horse we called "Snip," he was going down a side street running like a bat out of hell with about thirty feet of rope dragging. I wonder if they ever caught him.

After the three day hold up, which seemed like an eternity, we were all loaded . . . and headed back West, to "God's Country." The train pulled into Denver and the show broke up, Cowboys and Cowgirls scattering to the four winds from whence they came. Everyone was skeptical as to whether or not they would ever get what money they had coming or not, as there were lots of rodeos being promoted in those days that didn't have the proper financing behind them. If you worked one of them and it didn't pay off, you were just out. The Turtle Association hadn't come into being yet, demanding guaranteed purses for the contestants and stock contractors. Those rodeos that didn't pay off were called "Bloomers." I believe that everyone that had money coming from the Knights of Columbus was eventually paid. That is too fine an organization to leave anyone holding the sack for very long.[2]

During the year 1924, some of the other rodeos where Ike roped calves and won money were Uvalde, La Porte, and Houston, Texas, placing second at Houston. Others were Chicago, Illinois; Detroit, Michigan; Long Island and New York City, New York; and Boston, Massachusetts. Thousands of spectators attended all of these rodeos. The Sidney, Iowa, rodeo started in 1924, and a few years later was advertised as having the distinction of entertaining more spectators annually than any other four-day-and-night show of its kind in the United States. Ike went there consistently for the next several years.

Calf roping was new and was catching on. At first, ropers were tying calves like they had tied steers, bending over them to secure them. Ike would sit right down on them and squeeze their legs together with his short legs. This was another first in the rodeo world that Ike created, as this practice is the way calf roping developed and continues to this day. Ike was also the first to "leg" a calf to get it down, which involved grabbing the calf's front leg in order to throw it off balance so it would fall down. Considering calves weighed anywhere between 300 to 400 pounds in those early days, and Ike was of a smaller stature, this is the method he developed. It was told that at some of the indoor rodeos, mainly those held back East, sometimes the Brahma cross calves would have nubbin horns an inch or two long. This indicates the calves were big and heavy as their horns were already starting to grow on their head—and because the calves were so large, it was very difficult to pick up and throw them down the way it is done now. Ike's method of "legging a calf down" caught on for a while, but as the calves that were being used in rodeos became smaller over the years, this method became obsolete.

In 1925 Ike won Cheyenne in calf roping as well as the Douglas Fairbanks trophy saddle, just as he had promised his father he would when he was a very young boy. He'd won the Hoot Gibson Trophy at Prescott, Arizona, earlier that year in "calf tying"; the Prescott Humane Society would not let them flank and throw calves that year. Ike won a matched calf roping against Bob Crosby, one of the top ropers at that time, at Bartlesville, Oklahoma. Ike roped calves at Chandler and Fort Cobb, Oklahoma. He won the calf roping at Salt Lake City, Utah, and at Prescott, Arizona, and also won the team roping at Wickenburg and Tucson, Arizona, winning both first and second with different team roping partners.

THE WILD BUNCH

Vol. 8/No. 1   RODEO HALL OF FAME, OKLAHOMA CITY, OK   February 1986

TWO
IN-ONE
ISSUE
SEE
P. 18

An early 1920s photo of Ike standing next to Everett Bowman on a horse. It was featured on the February 1986 cover of *The Wild Bunch,* vol. 8, no. 1, Dickinson Research Center, National Cowboy and Western Heritage Museum.

Ike legging a calf, roping off Blue Darter at Tucson, Arizona, 1927. Notice the size of the calf.

Ike traveled around quite a bit of the country competing in rodeos in 1926, including: Safford, Arizona, where he team roped; then calf roped at Birmingham, Alabama, and St. Petersburg and Tampa, Florida, winning second at all of these. In Fort Stockton, Texas, he won first, and also roped in breakaway steer roping there. They did not trip the steer, just roped the animal around the horns, and then a string tied to the rope would break loose from the saddle horn when the steer reached the end of the rope. Ike also calf roped at Columbus, Ohio, and at Tucson, Arizona, winning second at both. At Ellensburg, Washington, he won first.

It was about this time that Ike set off on an ordinary enough adventure that turned deadly. Having arrived at the rodeo in Phoenix, Arizona, a few days early and then bumped into a cowboy he had worked with at the Double Circles before the war, Ike decided they should pay a visit to yet another of the cowboys they had both worked with some nine or ten years prior who was still working for the ranch. Horseback was the only way to get to this man's cow camp. The first friend said he would be happy to ride there with Ike to show him the way. What occurred after the two men arrived at the friend's camp turned into a deadly incident. While the three were visiting, two men broke into the shack. They had some sort of vendetta against the cowboy who lived there. (In Michael Grauer's history of the

Double Circles ranch, reproduced in appendix 2 of this book, he wrote that this ranch had a reputation for harboring outlaws. One of these two men could very well have been the outlaw Daniel "Red" Pipkin.) They forced the cowboy to drink a bottle of lye water they had brought with them. Immediately he went into convulsions and fell dead on the floor. They then turned to Ike and his friend and told them to drink the remaining contents in the bottle, as they didn't want any witnesses. Ike's friend drank first, then passed the bottle to Ike. Ike said there wasn't much left when the bottle was passed to him. He somehow faked that he was drinking most of it. The "outlaws" then left. Ike and his friend immediately got outside, where they vomited. They both managed to get on their horses. Ike went on to say that they had not ridden very far when his friend fell off his horse and died. Ike rode back down the mountain and reported the incident to a local sheriff. Though this thrilling tale was often repeated for us kids, my brother and I have forgotten some of the details like names and the exact location. However, we do know that Ike made it back to Phoenix to rope in the rodeo, but we don't know if he placed.

In 1927 he did win the calf roping at Phoenix, Arizona, and also at Fort Worth, Texas. Records show he placed in steer roping at Kiowa and Sedan, Kansas. All this time Ike was still matching Blue Darter in races held at the rodeos. This same year, the Texas State Fair in Dallas held the first known cutting horse contest for the public to pay to attend. Ike entered Blue Darter and won it! Darter was a proven racehorse, and people took notice. During one of Ike's trips to the Gardens in New York, a cowboy asked Ike what kind of horse he had. "I've got a war horse," said Ike, "and he can run, too."

"Would you want to match a race?" the guy asked.

"You're damn right," said Ike, "I'll run him at yours and drag a bale of hay. If that horse of yours ever gets a bite of it, you win!"

"How far do you want to run them, Ike?" the man asked.

"Any distance, from here to the Rocky Mountains," was Ike's reply.

In 1928 he again won calf roping at Sedan and Kiowa, Kansas. The years of 1927 and 1928 are short on documented records for where he roped, but he probably attended many more, such as known trips to Madison Square Garden, Cheyenne, and Detroit.

In 1929, Ike calf roped at Omaha and North Platte, Nebraska, Buffalo, Oklahoma, Canadian and San Antonio, Texas, where he won second. He won first at Cheyenne, Wyoming, again, and won the Stetson Trophy there. He also roped at Detroit, and Madison Square Garden, where he won a few go-rounds. That year, on Blue Darter, he won the calf roping at Calgary, Canada.

Ike calf roped in 1930 again at Detroit, as well as at Buckeye and Prescott, Arizona (third), San Diego, Texas (first), and he team roped at Prescott (coming in second).

In 1931 Ike calf roped at Saugus, California, where he won first, then Nampa, Idaho, Sidney, Iowa, and Ellensburg, Washington; and team roped at Livermore and Gilroy, California. That year he boarded a train and went to rope steers at Hermosillo, Sonora, Mexico. Ike won first day money on his first steer but his second steer out-ran him so he didn't place. He was riding Carl Arnold's horse Old Bill, as he didn't have Blue Darter with him.

Ike also won another Hoot Gibson Trophy at Prescott, Arizona, in calf roping in 1931. This year they were able to go back to flanking and throwing calves. Apparently they had settled their dispute with the Humane Society by then. He also steer roped at Cheyenne, Wyoming (second), and that year he won the prestigious steer roping at the Pendleton Round-Up in Oregon. There he won a Hamley saddle and his first leg on the Sam Jackson Trophy, a prestigious award given to the top All-Around Cowboy at Pendleton. His total money won there in both the steer roping and calf roping

Cowboys at Cheyenne in 1930: (*left to right*) Fred Lowry, Ike Rude, Mont Churchill, Richard Merchant, Jake McClure, and Bob Crosby.

Ike (*center*) sitting on his Hamley saddle, holding the Sam Jackson Trophy for winning the All-Around Cowboy title at Pendleton Round-Up, 1931. He is flanked by Mr. Hamley (*left*), and Burl Mulkey (*right*).

Cowboys at the Pendleton Round-Up: (*left to right*) Burl Mulkey, Ike Rude, Carl Arnold, Hugh Bennett, Jake McClure, King Merritt, and Tony Vey, 1931.

earned him the All-Around Cowboy award. To get this honor, a cowboy had to have won money in at least two events. At that time, there were no organizations or records kept of yearly earnings to determine who was the world champion for the year, but it was just understood—at least among the cowboys—that whoever won Pendleton, especially steer roping, would be considered the world champion. As for calf roping, it was still debatable as to whether the winner of Madison Square Garden or Pendleton should be called world champion.

As the photo of the saddle Ike won at Pendleton shows, it had some very expensive sterling silver on it. It was the most expensive saddle ever to be awarded to a cowboy champion at that time. Ike, having no use for the "shiny stuff," later took the silver off and sold it, but kept the saddle. He always loved to rope from a Hamley-made saddle.

At just thirty-seven years old in 1931, Ike had fulfilled his dream to be the best roper in the world! A newspaper clipping from the front page of the *East Oregonian* dated August 29, 1931, displays a bold headline in two-and-a-half-inches-tall letters proclaiming:

IKE RUDE IS WINNER, Oklahoma Roper Takes Sam Jackson Award in Stirring Arena Event

In the bright rays of a setting western sun, Ike Rude of Mangum, Oklahoma was crowned cowboy king at the close of the 1931 Round-Up this afternoon as winner of the Sam Jackson Trophy. Standing with Phil Jackson, Portland publisher, one of the donors of the trophy, Rude was handed the handsome sterling silver statue amidst the applause of thousands of spectators, who saw the last day's show.[3]

Somewhere along the way, Ike got dubbed with the nickname "Jitney," which was the name for a small bus back in the early 1900s that was advertised to "take you anywhere for 5 cents." Irby Mundy, a top Colorado roper, started calling Ike this and it stuck with him among the cowboys for his lifetime. Because of Ike's small stature and the way he traveled all over the country, the nickname just seemed to fit. And Ike did get around.

Traveling in 1932, he roped calves at Wolf Point, Montana, and made it to the big rodeos back East in Boston, Chicago, Philadelphia, and New York City. He team roped at Santa Maria, Ventura, and Los Angeles, California.

In 1933 Ike roped calves at Roswell, New Mexico, Memphis, Texas, and, as always, all the usual big shows back East that I have previously mentioned. From when Ike first started to rodeo, he would always compete at Madison Square Garden, Cheyenne Frontier Days, and Pendleton Round-Up, almost without fail.

And still, the rodeos listed are only a portion of the rodeos Ike attended. These are the ones that, years later, my mother had him remember so she could write them down in a journal to be kept all these years. The list included all those that he could recall winning any money at, so I do not know the ones he went to but didn't win, or that he couldn't remember. She did write the placings by a few that Ike had remembered, and where I have indicated the placing, I am referring to winning the average. For the other rodeos, I am assuming he won a part of the day money. And as much as Ike won, his focus wasn't only on the prize money.

When attendance was down at the 1933 World's Fair rodeo in Chicago, the rodeo promotors got with the cowboys and wondered if they could come up with an "added attraction" to help promote the rodeo and get people's attention. The cowboys came up with an idea, all right. They decided for a publicity stunt they would have a horse-swimming contest in Lake Michigan. While horseback, they would jump their horses off a barge and swim them to a designated point. Whoever made it there first was the winner. Ike would recall later that the water was awfully cold and that John Bowman and a bunch of his buddies nearly drowned. To make matters worse, the pick-up boats had a hard time getting the horses out of the water. Ike won the event, as he immediately slid back off Blue Darter's rump, held him by the tail, and kept splashing water on each side of his eyes so he would go in the direction of the finish line. Some of the other cowboys tried to stay in the saddle, but this didn't work well at all. Ike's prior experience crossing rivers while employed on the big ranches paid off on this stunt! Years later, when rodeo writer and historian Willard Porter asked Ike if he won the race, Ike's reply was, "I sure did. Don't forget that I had plenty of practice swimming the Red River before I ever got to Lake Michigan . . . There's not many of us left who can say that." A photo of the starting line shows that the wild stunt certainly pulled in lots of spectators. Look at the photo of all the spectators that were in attendance!

Cowboys jumping horses off a barge for a race in Lake Michigan, which Ike won. Ike on Blue Darter, wearing a black hat. Dick Truitt in front. Worlds Fair Rodeo, Chicago, 1933. Photo courtesy of Old Greer County Museum and Hall of Fame, Mangum, Oklahoma.

Appreciation came in other forms as well:

> At the World's Fair rodeo in Chicago, at an invitational affair in 1933, a bunch of the boys were guests of the Swift family of the Swift Packing Company, on their Lake Forest estate for several days. Ida Mae Swift and her husband took a real liking to Darter and tried to buy him for their daughter. Ike wouldn't sell, but he got to thinking. Darter was showing his age, he was 21 years old, and Ike knew he was sure indebted to the horse and he'd never find a "plushier" home for the old fellow to spend the rest of his days, and likely he'd never have the horse back in that part of the country again. So, at the conclusion of the rodeo, though there were still some miles in the old campaigner, Ike gave Blue Darter to the Swift Family.[4]

What a horse—from being just "the Hog Horse" in his early years, Blue Darter became one of the best all-around roping horses of his time on goats, calves, steers, and in team roping. He was also a short distance race horse, had won a swimming contest in Lake Michigan, was the big winner of the first cutting horse contest at the State Fair of Texas, not to mention a roping horse that Will Rogers would have paid anything to own. All this plus being Ike's transportation for thousands of miles to and from the ropings and rodeos prior to cars and horse trailers! I would say the horse sure enough earned his keep. If records had been kept during that time, Darter should have been put in the halls of fame alongside Ike's future horses that were so honored. Of course, this was before any such organization had been formed and before anyone kept records of winnings or accomplishments, so Blue Darter was never enshrined. What also comes to mind as I write of his achievements is that this horse was used so very hard for so many years yet apparently never had any serious lameness or went sour. Ike usually shod and treated his own horses if they did get sick. Lots of old remedies were handed down from cowboys working the ranches, so Ike knew how to treat a horse if it got sick, and of course it was a requirement for cowboys to know how to keep their horses shod. The horses that are shown today, at horse shows at least, have to have chiropractors and all sorts of veterinary work to keep them sound. Blue Darter was hauled a *lot* as well as having been ridden hundreds of miles on the ranches plus more to the rodeos for many years, then hauled from one end of the United States to the other and back again several times, and used in a very physical way. He did not even have the comfort of the nice horse trailers that are used today. I think this speaks highly of the horseman that Ike was and of the special care he gave to this horse and to the many more that were to come in his future.

EIGHT

London, England, 1934

Tex Austin produced a rodeo in London, England, in 1924, but the British people did not accept the production warmly. This rodeo consisted of several specialty acts, women bronc riders, trick and fancy roping, as well as bronc riding and calf roping. After the first rodeo was held in London, the Royal Society for Prevention of Cruelty to Animals obtained a court order prohibiting the shows, which was lifted after Tex assured the authorities that calf roping would be eliminated.

In 1934, Tex Austin staged another rodeo in England. He recruited the top American cowboys and cowgirls to go to England and perform in this rodeo. Ike and the other calf ropers that agreed to go were under the impression that the ban on calf roping had been lifted. However, once they arrived, they were informed that they could only "break-away" rope: once the calf was roped, the rope had to break away. Thus the calf is never jerked or tied down.

The *Fort Worth Star Telegram* reported the following about this rodeo going to England:

ABOARD THE AURANIA, enroute to London.

After turning staid old Montreal into a city of Western atmosphere, 125 cowgirls and cowboys are aboard the Aurania, going to London for the Tex Austin World Championship Rodeo. Many of the contestants and officials are from Fort Worth. [Later there were reports that about 200 cowboys and cowgirls made the trip to London so apparently more had joined the group for which this writer was unaware.]

Greeted, welcomed and "stared-at" the rodeo outfit spent three days in Montreal, sailing point and concentration center for the contestants coming from 13 of the United States and several provinces of Canada.

Two days before the boat sailed with most of the contestants, 450 head of rodeo livestock were placed aboard a freighter for a voyage. Thirty cowboys and a veterinarian were aboard to care for the animals. Stalls, spotlessly clean, had been arranged for them on the boat.

Crowd Watches Loading.

At daybreak a crowd began to assemble to see the animals placed aboard the Nortonian. A long runway, leading from a train to the boat had been built and cautiously the bucking broncs made their way to their "cabins." Even "Five Minutes to Midnight," one of the roughest of bucking horses, made little protest as he approached the last section of the runway which was so steep that some of the horses skidded down it.

Throughout the six hours required for the loading of the animals on the boat the crowds came. Then two days later when the Aurania left with the contestants a throng crowded around the gangplanks to see a "real cowboy."

Numerous newspapers had reporters and cameramen present. Talkie movies were made. It was a day of excitement for Montreal—as well as for the contestants, many of whom are known to the audiences of the Southwestern Exposition and Fat Stock Show.

Due in London May 27.

The boat carrying the contestants is scheduled to reach London May 27. Before it docks it will have passed the Nortonian, carrying the livestock.

The departure of the livestock boat brought temporary separation for several wives and husbands as no women were allowed to sail on the cattle boat. A cameraman snapped a photo Louis Kubit of Fort Worth kissing his bride of a month goodbye. They will meet again in London.

News reached the boat that the House of Lords had passed a law against the staging of rodeos in England, because of "cruelty to animals." However, the rodeo officials do not believe that it will interfere in any manner with the staging of the rodeo in London because of a treaty with the United States which provides that England cannot make laws that can be applied retroactively to contracts previously made. The Tex Austin contract was signed months ago.

Montreal Papers Tell.

The rodeo likely will be taken to Scotland and several other European countries.

Here is the way one Montreal newspaper referred to the arrival of the cowboys:

Windsor Street lost its staid atmosphere yesterday and was turned into a rip-snortin' western "drag" when the bronc bucking boys from Texas and other States hit town. Big-hatted, leathery faced men of the saddle has transformed the district around the Queen's Hotel—their temporary headquarters—into a scene of one of Zane Grey's novels.

They'll be leaving tomorrow, 125 of them, off for London to Tex Austin's Rodeo, but in the meantime they are giving Montrealers something to look at. There were big doings yesterday. Lanky riders from Texas and other States grasped hands with drawling cowboys from Alberta, Canada and there was a thunder and wheeling of "Howdy partner" and "Shore glad to see yuh."

These are the men who make women shriek when they go down in dust and dirt hugging a steer's horns. These are the human cocktail-shakers who bounce around on a horse's back. As one wiry, brown-faced young champion put it, "We shore don't worry much about reducin' exercises."

Hats Blot Out Sun.

They shore don't need 'em.

When they get in a group with their big hats, the sun may have set for all you know about it. And when they start tramping along the streets in their high-heeled boots, it sounds something like a Buffalo stampede.

And some of them will be World Champions when they get back from Europe.

Newspapers at cities through which the special train went, carried such headlines as: "Western Cowboys Invade Montreal," "Bedlam Reigns as Cowboys Play at Union Station," "Rodeo Bound for England," and "Cowhands Go to Freighter to Bid Livestock Farewell."

At Detroit, the poet, Edgar A. Guest, who writes "Just Folks," greeted the cowhands. He posed for a picture with pretty Lucyle Roberts of Antlers, Oklahoma. "My how I wish I was going on this trip," he said.[1]

The entourage of the Tex Austin-produced rodeo heading to London was a news headline in both the United States and Canada and, as the above writing shows, was quite sensationalized.

After reaching London, Ike wrote a letter home to his mother:

June 4, 1934,

Dear Mother, I am here in England, had a wonderful trip, sailed from Montreal, Canada, May 16th, landed at Cardiff, Wales, stayed there four days and then came here, to London. I sure had a good time in Wales, that is the prettiest country I ever saw. The people were just grand to us. I was lucky, a millionaire and race horse man kept me out at his estate nearly all the time, and he is one of the wealthiest in England, (so they say). A big shot took 4 or 5 of us out to White Country England, 65 miles from here, yesterday and showed us where the Thorobred's home is. That is, I mean, where the good horses are raised in this country. They were wonderful to us, had a big dinner and everything. We are going places most every day. I got here with my horse alright, he is in good shape. These old humane people

Cowboys on ship in the middle of the Atlantic Ocean, on their way to the London rodeo, 1934. Ike is on the left with a rope in hand, always ready to rope something.

are giving us trouble over here. They don't want us to rope calves and jerk them down, so I guess we will rope them and break loose with a string at the horn of the saddle. I don't care, just so we get to rope and I guess we will alright. The money is all up in the bank and everything. I feel as tho I have got a good chance to make some money here. We were 10 days on the ocean. I wasn't sick a bit. I saw 3 icebergs a day or so out of Montreal; one looked as large as a mountain. It was about a mile from us. This sure has been a wonderful trip. I am coming home to see you without fail inside of the next 3 months. How are all the folks, give them all my best, tell Dad I am having a wonderful time. Write to me right away, London, England, care of White City Stadium.

Your boy, Ike . . .
P. S. Lots of girls over here!

During Ike's trip to London, the Queen of England requested her own special performance by the cowboys. Ike calf roped at this performance for the royals at White City Stadium.

Willard Porter wrote about what Ike told him of the rodeo in London: "The English people never took to our rodeos much, but the main trouble was those old tough horses. The English people thought, you know, that the King's Stable riders were the best. They came out . . . three or four of them did . . . and got in the bronc riding . . . and those horses near killed them all. American cowboys were carrying 'em off the field as fast as they could. Englishmen had never seen anything like it and they were mad."[2] The rodeo was far too wild and cruel for the English. They did not appreciate any part of it.

England's *Daily Herald* reported:

Animals being sold to meet expenses. Cowboys leave for home "disgusted" by lack of support. More than 200 American and Canadian cowgirls and cowboys were leaving England on this day. 300 wild horses and steers were being sold as rapidly as possible in order that the National Sporting Club might be able to recoup money that they had backed by endorsing this event. The bucking horses and cow ponies that were privately owned by the cowboys and cowgirls were put on a boat and shipped back to the United States.[3]

Tex Austin suffered a financial disaster and was unable to pay the contestants. Broke, blue, and homesick, all the cowboys were wondering how they were going to get home from London. Ike always kept his sense of humor, even in critical times. He was standing at the train station, waiting for the train, even though he was broke and didn't have a dime to his name. Dick Truitt, an Oklahoma cowboy, and Hugh Bennett, a Colorado cowboy, both friends of Ike's, were there also. Hugh would recall in his book *Horseman, Brand of a Legend* how Ike began his journey home:

> Why, there he [Ike] sat on his suitcase. He'd packed his suitcase, and he got his clothes all in but one leg of his Levis. It was hangin' out. I saw that train comin' way down the tracks, and there was Dick Truitt standin' there. I said, "Ike how you gonna get home?" "Hell, I'm waitin for a cottonwood log to drift by so's I can catch it and get home!" he said. So I said, "Dick, grab one arm and his suitcase, and we'll throw him on the train." So when the first door came open, we threw the suitcase in; then when the next door came open, we threw him in. He had no money.
>
> There was an old greyhound dog there that had just outrun everybody, and they couldn't get him matched. His name was Veal Cutlets. So they gave him to Bob Askins, [one of the cowboys from the United States that competed in saddle bronc riding] and Askins was on this train, but Ike didn't know that when we threw him on. So when they got into France, they found out about the dog races, and they took Veal Cutlets. He won them enough money to get something to eat on the way home.[4]

Their ship took them to Montreal, Canada, and from there the cowboys took a train to Cheyenne, Wyoming.

NINE

Bullet, 1934–1942

The Great Depression stretched from 1929 to 1939, but, ironically, those years were some of the easiest times for Ike to make money roping. It was no problem for him to win.

After returning from England in 1934 at forty years old, Ike got his first car and learned to drive. For a long period of time, his mode of transportation was either riding his horse to the closer shows or he and his horse would board a train. In the middle to latter 1920s, after horse trailers were becoming fairly common, he would hitch a ride for himself and horse, traveling with Barton Carter or some other cowboy who might have a horse trailer. Ike was still taking trains while others were using cars and trailers. That all changed after he went with Barton to a rodeo at Indianapolis, Indiana. Ike must have had a big win, because he decided it was time to buy an automobile and learn to drive. After the rodeo, the two cowboys went out to the Indianapolis Speedway, and for the next hour or so Barton showed Ike how to drive a car "on the Speedway." After this, Ike bought his own horse trailer and his own "rig" and didn't have to hitch a ride anymore.

During the years 1933 and 1934 Ike roped calves at Roswell, New Mexico, Memphis, Texas, New Harmony, Indiana, Chicago, Illinois, Sidney, Iowa. and Madison Square Garden, to name a few. He team roped at Santa Maria, Ventura, and Los Angeles, California. These are the only ones that are recorded, but there were many others.

After retiring Blue Darter, Ike owned a horse he calf roped on from 1933 to 1935 that was called Roany, but the next great roping horse he owned was Bullet. Like Blue Darter, Bullet was of Peter McCue breeding. He was raised by Hoyt Lewis of House, New Mexico. A grandson of Peter McCue, his sire was Jack McCue and his dam was a little Thoroughbred mare. The Lewis boys, Roy and Pat, themselves top-hand ropers, trained Bullet for calf roping when he was still a young horse. They had been winning on the little horse when they sold him to Bob Crosby, one of the top ropers at that time. After Bob purchased him, he started training him on steer roping. He had just had him a short while when it was time to go to Cheyenne to the Frontier Days.

At Cheyenne in 1935, Ike's horse went sour (meaning he just quit working) and let him down in the first run. Bob Crosby had brought Bullet, a seven-year-old gelding, with him to Cheyenne. Bob also had another horse

Ike on Roany, his calf roping horse after he gave Blue Darter to the Swift family, at Chicago, 1934.

he was steer roping on. He told Ike that he was welcome to rope his next go-round on Bullet, but the horse was fairly green, so he hadn't had a lot of training in steer roping. Ike roped his next steer on him and he knew he had to buy the horse. Bob agreed to sell Bullet to Ike. Ike found his old buddy King Merritt and told him they should partner to buy him. The two best friends did just that. After the Cheyenne rodeo, they took him to King's ranch at Federal, Wyoming, and proceeded with fine-tuning his training. The first rodeo they took him to was the Pendleton Round-Up, where, between the two of them roping on him, they won $1,700. King won first in the steer roping and Ike was second. They figured they had made a very good investment. The following year at Pendleton, Ike won the steer roping on him and also won his second leg on the 1936 Sam Jackson Trophy, the traveling trophy awarded to the top All-Around Cowboy at the Round-Up. He also won another Hamley saddle there.

> During the years that Ike was on Bullet, he was a hard cowboy to beat. He won or placed at nearly every steer roping he went to, and at Pryor, Oklahoma, one year he roped, tripped, and tied a long-horned critter in a flat 16. "And those were the days," Ike said, "when steers were cattle, not a bunch of old goats. When I was riding Bullet, most of the steers I roped weighed 960 to 1,020 pounds. And as small as he was, old Bullet made those cattle look puny. He was fast and ran hard when you caught one and threw a trip."[1]

Bullet never weighed over 960 pounds and only stood 14.2 hands tall, or 4 feet, 10 inches.

> Once Merritt had seen him drag a 1600 pound bull out of the arena at Fort Worth. Merritt described Bullet, the "biggest little horse I ever saw." He had a talent for handling big cattle. The horse had to beat the steer to the draw, and Bullet had a way in doing that. He had an act in getting away from a steer that no other horse had. It was kind of a fade away feeling, and when he turned his tail to a steer, all you had to do was be on the ground in position to hogtie, as he would drag him to you so fast that you would think he was going clear out of the arena with him, for he would pick up speed after you hit the ground, but never did he drag over one foot too far or one foot too short. He carried many a cowboy to the pay window, as he always had from three to five ropers on him at most shows.[2]

Bullet was the best steer roping horse going down the road. Ike and King were making money hand over fist by roping off him. They also allowed many of the top cowboys, for a percentage of their winnings, to rope off him. Steers that were roped in those days were much larger than steers in recent years, and it was very physically rough on a horse to take the jerk, especially a little horse, but Bullet seemed to be a natural at knowing how to position himself.

Ike always said Bullet was probably the best steer horse that ever was, and a lot of other cowboys thought so, too, as the horse's reputation was passed down over generations, and years later, in 1979, the horse was inducted into the ProRodeo Hall of Fame.

In 1937, Ike sold his half-interest in Bullet to King for $600, but retained a seat on him, being able to rope on him anytime. He continued to steer rope on him, but in 1936 he had purchased another horse, primarily for calf roping, that would make the both of them truly famous.

In 1938, while roping on Bullet, Ike won the average at Woodward, Oklahoma, and was awarded the Jim Selman rodeo trophy for the outstanding

Ike on Bullet at a rodeo in Woodward, Oklahoma, 1938.

cowboy of the three-day rodeo. Ike would go on to win the steer roping there again in 1940, 1952, and 1954.

In 1941 Ike won the steer roping at Cheyenne, Wyoming. He also won his first "official" World Champion Steer Roping title on Bullet, as an organization had finally been formed to officially record yearly winnings. Whoever won the most accumulated money for the year was declared the world champion. This is how the world champion in each event is still determined today. The following year, 1942, King Merritt did the same, with Ike winning second behind King for World Steer Roping Champion.

During this time, while Ike was staying in a hotel during a rodeo at Elko, Nevada, someone stole from his room two suitcases full of belt buckles he had won. After that, if Ike won a buckle, he would keep the one he liked the most to wear for himself, but give the rest away. Material things only proved to be problems for Ike's nomadic lifestyle.

THE COWBOYS TURTLE ASSOCIATION

At the 1936 Madison Square Garden rodeo, Ike was approached by his good friend Hugh Bennett about joining a new organization. This organization addressed some of the cowboy contestants' concerns regarding the many problems that the contestants were having, like more uniform livestock, money being distributed among the events more fairly, advertisement of upcoming rodeos, reporting of rodeo win results, as well as a better judging system for the judged events. One of the rules of this new organization was that a "professional cowboy" could not compete in, or even attend, any "amateur" rodeo or there would be a large fine to pay. This, Hugh felt, would serve to keep the "professionals" as such. Though Hugh was the brains behind this organization that would become the Cowboys Turtle Association (CTA), Hugh quickly recruited Everett Bowman to become president, with Hugh as secretary/treasurer. Josie Bennett, Hugh's wife, would end up being the workforce behind the scenes: she kept track of all monies and the reporting of all event winnings from the back seat of her car for many years. Hugh thought the perfect place to get organized was that year at the Garden rodeo.

As mentioned previously in the "Brief History of Rodeo," rodeo producer Colonel W. T. Johnson had a contract with both New York's Madison Square Garden and the immediately following Boston Garden rodeos. The Colonel was not distributing the money fairly among the different events.

He was giving a more sizeable amount to the trick roping and trick riding events. In the calf roping, he was not even adding the cowboys' entry fees to the purse in order to include more money in a larger payout—he was just paying them an amount that he would determine. The ropers and even the bronc riders were not being paid much for their competition winnings, either.

Hugh Bennett wrote in his book *Horseman, Brand of a Legend*:

> Colonel W. T. Johnson, one of the greatest producers of rodeo who had more class than any man before or since . . . So there in New York, I tried to get Mr. Johnson to add the entry fee to the purse. But he wanted it all. He was a shrewd old fellow. We were paying him to let us work! We were putting up our own purse! So I jumped him there in New York, and told him that if I had my car and trailer here, I'd go home to Arizona from here in New York 'cause you can't make any money, not a chance.

Most of the cowboys had traveled to New York and the Boston Gardens on Col. Johnson's rodeo train and did not have a means to get home without riding his train. The cowboys planned a strike: they would not perform at the Boston Gardens if their demands were not met.

> We went on over to Boston and were there about a week before the show. We started on the Turtles Association, having meetings two or three times a day, sometimes four. We made our rules and regulations and everyone signed the petition. After this snow job, ol' man Johnson gave me the last night before we left New York. Josie and I were walking across the street from the Garden to the Belvadere Hotel and I said, "Honey, I'm goin' to see Richard Merchant in the morning and get him to sell all these boys a ticket to get back home because he's accustomed to handling all these party movements. We'll have our own train ready to leave Boston at midnight if this strike doesn't work." A lot of people thought that we walked out on the old man there in Boston, but he came down there about 2 o'clock, and none of us had entered. He came around the corner of the office there and he saw me and said, "Get these damned horses out of this Garden!" I'd made arrangements up the street there a couple of blocks to keep our horses there until midnight. But we had them saddled up then. I had a pack on old Hazel Eyes, had everything in the world on that

old horse. Hazel Eyes was an old roping horse. Johnson said, "Get 'em out of here!" 'Cause he wasn't going to have us dictate to him how to run his show. I said, "We're waiting for the press." Just about that time the press showed up, and they got a picture of us going out of the Garden. Came out an extra in the paper that night; "NO RODEO… COWBOYS GOING TO ARIZONA."

The first night of the Boston Garden rodeo, the cowboys went on strike and did not compete. The striking cowboys had purchased tickets to the rodeo and were sitting up in the stands watching it. The bucking horses were bucking all the cowboys right off and in the calf roping many were not getting their calf roped. Most all of the top riders and ropers were on strike—not in the competition. The cowboys, as well as the majority of the crowd, were booing and shouting. They were not happy with the quality of performances that night.

So Mr. Johnson had the announcer ask us to come down in the arena. We marched down there in the arena and he said, "Now what do you want?" I said, "G-damn, we been talking about what we want. We don't want a damned thing from you; we just want our entry fee added to the purse." They gave everybody back their ticket. The rodeo was a failure. They didn't have a show. Mr. Johnson said, "Well I'm agreeable to that."

A contract was then written up to verify the agreement.

So the announcer told the people that this was a rain out, and to come back the next night and we would have a normal show . . . You know that old boy Johnson sold out that night to Gene Autry, The Clemens Brothers from Arizona, and Everett Colburn from Texas. We never did see the Colonel any more. He meant what he said. He wasn't going to be dictated to. I feel awful proud to have started the Association. There wasn't any way that his snow job could go on, for there wasn't anyone making any money except old man Johnson.[3]

Ike would be #57 to join the Cowboys Turtle Association.

Ike steer roping on Bullet at the Pendleton Round-Up, 1941.

Picture taken at the McAlester, Oklahoma, prison rodeo, sometime in the late 1930s or early 1940s. (*Left to right*) Ike Rude, Ace Soward (Ike's brother-in-law), John McEntire (Clark McEntire's father and Reba McEntire's grandfather), the prison warden, and Floyd Gale.

Ike always felt that if rodeos would have reported all their results from 1929 to 1937, he would have won about three world championships in calf roping during this period. As noted, the results of rodeos were not always in compliance with the RAA by-laws during the early 1930s. After the Cowboys Turtle Association was formed, records were better kept.

RECOLLECTIONS

Many years later while visiting with Lanham Riley, who was a top calf and steer roper in the 1940s and '50s, talk came around to the subject of Dad's horses. Lanham told me that Ike was the first roper he knew of that wanted, and had, a strong bloodline of Thoroughbred breeding in his roping horses. Ike felt it was essential for the speed and endurance in a roping horse. All of Ike's horses had a top Thoroughbred in their pedigree, and not very far back in their lineage.

TEN

Ike Gets Roped and Tied, 1937

Cleo Crouch was born April 14, 1918, the youngest of five children of George and Amy Crouch of Buffalo, Oklahoma. George had homesteaded his ranch with the 1889 Land Run of Oklahoma, and from 1920 to 1930 had produced one of the earliest rodeos in the surrounding area that included northwestern Oklahoma, the panhandle of Texas, southern Kansas, and southeastern Colorado. It was the Doby Springs Rodeo, which was held just west of the present town of Buffalo. Ike had attended this rodeo off and on over the years.

Cleo was no stranger to the ranch and rodeo world. She had been riding horses, bringing in the milk cows, and helping around the ranch on horseback with various other chores, including cooking for the ranch hands, for most of her life. Every year, Cleo helped her family put on the Doby Springs Rodeo.

The fourth child born to George and Amy Crouch was a boy, Glen Crouch. He, too, worked on ranches all his life, and he roped calves for a short time in the early 1930s. In 1937 his calf roping at Madison Square Garden won enough money to come home and buy himself a car and purchase a diamond ring to give to his fiancé, Inez. However, Inez did not wish to be traveling all over the country, so from then on Glen worked on ranches and gave up rodeos. Years later, Glen would tell his children about riding on the train with his horse to New York and how they, the cowboys, would ride in the stock car with them. Also he would tell about eating with the hobos while traveling.

The third child, Twila, married Ace Soward, a prominent steer and calf roper and steer wrestler in the late 1920s through around 1950 who was also from Buffalo. Ace was a force to be reckoned with in those years of roping.

He placed in several of the top rodeos, however he never won first in a major rodeo. Ace was one of the members of the Cowboys Turtle Association.

The second child, Neva, married an insurance man and rancher by the name of Harry Carlisle. Neva is the only one of the Crouch children who, after marrying, never was involved in rodeos.

The oldest of the Crouch children, Opal, married Monte Reger. When they were married, Mr. Crouch gave them a longhorn steer as a wedding gift. George had purchased this steer because he was unusual in that he had a beautiful set of matched horns on him. Monte trained the steer to be ridden and to jump over cars. Monte and Opal eventually traveled all over the United States to rodeos and fairs to perform and do exhibitions. The steer was affectionately called "Bobby" by the Crouch family, short for his stage name "Bobcat Twister." Bobby provided their family a living for the next several years. His legacy is now preserved in story and in taxidermy in the National Cowboy and Western Heritage Museum in Oklahoma City. Monte and Opal had three children: Virginia, Buddy, and Dixie, all of whom, at a very young age, became trick riders and ropers at rodeos throughout the nation, performing with their father, Monte, and Bobcat Twister. Monte also was a rodeo announcer.

Monte and Opal's youngest, daughter Dixie, was quite a good calf roper and trick rider herself at a very young age, and was the first girl rodeo clown. Dixie has since been inducted into the National Cowgirl Hall of Fame in Fort Worth, Texas, in the year 1982 and also into the National Rodeo Hall of Fame in Oklahoma City in 2003. Dixie helped organize the Girls Rodeo Association (GRA), that would later be renamed to the Women's Professional Rodeo Association (WPRA).

Their middle child, Virginia, would later marry Tom Hadley, a prominent rodeo announcer. Virginia continued trick riding and roping for several years into her marriage. She would later be inducted in the "Texas Cowboy Hall of Fame."

The oldest child was Monte Dean, but went by the nickname "Buddy." He would grow up to be a rodeo clown and announcer for a time, and then helped his Dad, Monte, in the Livestock Sale Barn at Woodward, Oklahoma, for many years.

In 1937, the youngest of George and Amy Crouch's children, Cleo, turned nineteen. She entered a beauty contest at Woodward, Oklahoma,

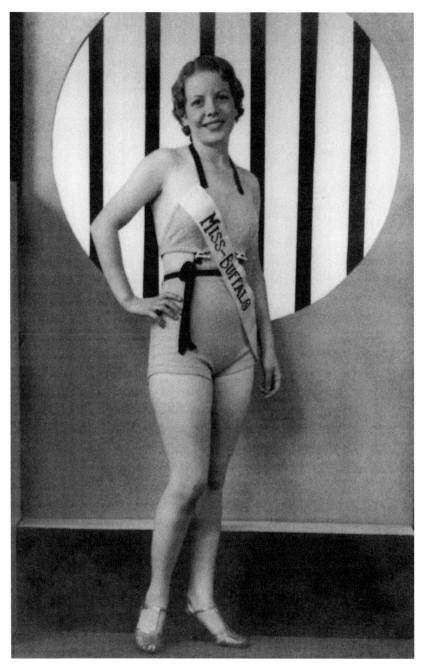

1937, Cleo Crouch, Miss Buffalo.

where she was awarded second place and a free session at a studio to have her photograph taken in her swimsuit. Following this contest, she entered the Northwest Oklahoma Beauty Contest and won first. That same year, Cleo was chosen to be "Miss Buffalo" and to represent the town of Buffalo as a rodeo queen contestant at the Oklahoma State Fair, held in Oklahoma City.

By 1937, Mr. Crouch had passed away and Ace Soward was running the ranch for his mother-in-law, Amy Crouch. Ike and Ace had become friends and occasional traveling companions to rodeos. They traveled together this particular time to a rodeo at Guymon, Oklahoma, in May 1937. On Ike's way back to Pawhuska, still his hangout in between his layover times on the road, Ace asked Ike and his other traveling buddy, Chock Dyer, to spend a night at the ranch before going on, which Ike readily accepted.

When they drove up to the ranch house, Ike saw a pretty young woman coming out of the house and asked Ace who that was. Ace replied that was his wife's younger sister, Cleo. Ike was immediately interested and told Ace he wanted to meet her. Ace replied that he would introduce him, but for Ike to not get any ideas as she was engaged to be married. Ike's reply was, "Engaged don't make me any difference, I want to marry her!" They hadn't even met yet! Ace then introduced Ike to Cleo Crouch.

After supper, Cleo said Ike followed her around like a puppy dog. He helped her clear the dishes and kept coming into the kitchen wanting to help. "Every time I would turn around, I would bump into him," Cleo would share years later. The next day Cleo went swimming in a big galvanized tin stock tank kept behind the ranch house for just that purpose. Ike borrowed some swimming trunks from Ace (Ace was a very big man and Ike was several sizes smaller, but somehow Ike made them work by tying a rope around the waist). Another problem was that Ike had no beach shoes. So here he comes out of the house to join her with these borrowed swimming trunks on, many sizes too big, and wearing his cowboy boots. Don't you know that sight would impress a girl!

Well, something must have worked for Ike, because by the next week or two, he sent Cleo a telegram. The stationmaster at Buffalo called to tell her that he was in receipt of a telegram from Ike Rude and she needed to come to town to pick it up. She didn't know when she could make a trip into town from the ranch, so she requested it be read to her on the phone. The stationmaster told her it was rather personal, that she might not want it read over the telephone's party line. But Cleo told him to go ahead and read it anyway. The telegram said: "I love you and always will. Write me in care of Chock Dyer, Bartlesville, Ike." It had been sent from Pawhuska, just a few miles from Bartlesville. Shortly thereafter Cleo broke her engagement to the other guy.

Ike proposed to Cleo just a few months later. They were married November 18, 1937, at the home of Cleo's sister and brother-in-law, Monte and Opal Reger, at Woodward, Oklahoma. Cleo was nineteen, Ike was forty-three years old. There were twenty-four years' difference in their ages. Don't you know that was a scandal! It must have been the talk of Buffalo, Oklahoma. Ike told Cleo that he would show her all over the country, their travels would take them everywhere. This must have sounded very exciting to Cleo, as she had only been away from home once in her life, and that was to visit her married sister, Neva, who lived in Mississippi. Ike Rude was already a roping legend, and was in the prime of his career. After the ceremony, they immediately took off for a rodeo at Tucson, Arizona.

Ike's bachelor days had finally come to an end.

ELEVEN

Baldy, 1936–1942

n 1936, Ike and King Merritt still owned Bullet and both were winning in steer roping while riding him, as well as mounting several of the other steer ropers on him. The horse was being used a lot. Ike was on the search for another horse that he could use in addition to Bullet, mainly for calf roping. Ike found his next great horse at Ronald Mason's Cross J Ranch at Nowata, Oklahoma. It was a horse that would become one of the most famous and immortalized roping horses of all time.

Mr. Mason had purchased a yearling colt from his neighbor John Dawson, whose ranch was at Talala, Oklahoma. The chestnut colt was born in 1932. His sire was Old Red Buck and his dam was Babe Dawson. By the time Ike saw him, the horse was a three-year-old gelding. He had already been broke and had started his training in roping calves by Louis Brooks, a cowboy who was working for Mason at this time. In the years to follow, Brooks became a top saddle bronc rider.

> One day, after starting Baldy on calves, Brooks said to Mason, "This one's got a heck of a stop. Watch and I'll show you." After Brooks roped a calf and pitched his slack, he hollered "Whoa," at which time Baldy promptly applied the brakes. Brooks flew over the saddle horn and hit the ground like a sack of cement. Mason chuckled and said, "Louis, it looks to me like he's got too good a stop."[1]

The horse weighed about 1,070 pounds. Ike liked what he saw in him and bought a half-interest in him from Mr. Mason for $200. Ike named him "Baldy," or sometimes referred to as "Ol' Baldy" because of the wide white marking that ran down his head. Ike immediately went to finish training him for calf roping. "After Ike purchased the horse, he further tempered the bald-faced sorrel's stop. Often, he would tie one end of a rope to a heavy, three-cornered harrow and the other to his saddle horn. He then faced Baldy to the plow, tugged the reins and squalled, Back, Baldy! The gelding would then bury his rear deeply to move the heavy plow."[2]

> That winter, 1936, Mr. Mason rode out to the rodeo at Tucson, Arizona with Ike and Ike talked him out of the other half interest. Tucson was Baldy's first big rodeo. The score line then was at one hundred feet and calves weighed over four hundred pounds. They had four go-rounds. Ike would have won the average in the calf roping, but on the last calf, the calf came out of the chute and then stopped at the score line. Ike was chasing him at such a fast pace, in order to make up the hundred foot head start the calf had, and Baldy ran right over the top of the calf, knocking Ike out of his win.[3]

Ike also entered in the team roping there that year on Baldy. They were roping "hard and fast." In fact he was entered on Baldy with four different partners.

> Years later, in an interview with Willard Porter for his book, *Roping and Riding*, Ike was asked if Old Baldy's stop was natural or a result of his schooling. He replied, "Oh, I'm sure it was both. Baldy was a real athlete . . . he had the right moves. But I'll tell you this, Willard, I don't think he ever forgot the first team tying I took him to at Tucson, Arizona. You remember they used to have a one hundred-foot score there and that year the steers must have weighed eight hundred pounds. I was roping with four different partners—Buckshot [Sorrells], the old Mexican heeler, [Tony Altamirano] and a couple of others. I broke a rope on my first steer, but after that we roped and tied down every one. Baldy got used to that weight and just plumb stuck his legs into the sod to get ready for the shock. A lot of weight puts a stop on 'em."[4]

Early competition team roping started out in California and Arizona. There were two kinds. One was "tie-down team roping," which was sometimes referred to as "hard and fast team roping," where the ropes were tied fast onto the saddle horn by both header and heeler. After both the horns and the heels were roped by the team, with horses facing away from the steer to stretch him out, the header would then dismount and run back to tie the hind-legs of the steer together before the time would be stopped. This type of team roping was first and mainly performed in Arizona. The other type of team roping, "dally team roping," was where header and healer dally their ropes around the saddle horn after respectively catching the horns and heels of the steer, then turn their horses to face the steer and the time stops. The header never dismounts from his horse to tie the steer. This was the form being done in California. Over the years the tie-down team roping style was abolished as once again the Humane Society thought this was too rough on the stock. Dally team roping has since taken over the whole United States and has become the most popular roping event of them all.

Ike entered Baldy in matching horse races as well. Ike was quoted as saying, "I'll match him the length of a corn cob, or to the Rocky Mountains." Once at Imperial, California, Ike entered him in a horse race there that attracted many of the top race horses that had been winning at the tracks in that part of the country. Ol' Baldy won it handily. Ike said, "He day-lighted them by several horse lengths."

There have been several articles speculating why Baldy had such an outstanding and abrupt stop when roping calves. Whatever it was, it is for certain that before he was ever roped off from, that stop was just something that horse naturally did. It was developed even more as Ike roped more cattle on him. Ike was once asked how he trained a horse to rate a cow, meaning how to train a horse to follow but not run over the cow, staying just behind the cow and following it, allowing a cowboy to get as close as possible to rope it. Ike's reply was that he never pulled on a horse during this process. He let the horse figure it out for himself. A good horse will do this. He went on to say, "A horse knows what a man knows. You can't teach a horse something you don't know yourself. You can take about any horse and train them, some learn better than others, but you can't put the 'speed' in one. That is something that has to be bred in them."

In 1936, Ike on Baldy won the calf roping at Elko, Nevada. He also had a third-place win in calf roping at Winnemucca, Nevada. Ike had the best calf roping horse of the times, and he was mounting a lot of other cowboys on him also, or at least those who could ride him when he stopped. Ike and Baldy were a team to be reckoned with in calf roping and then, in August of that year, tragedy hit. Ike and a traveling buddy, Junior Caldwell, had been at a rodeo in Winnipeg, Canada. They were traveling back through Nebraska headed for the Burwell rodeo, towing Baldy in a horse trailer, when Ike's buddy tossed a cigarette out the window of the moving car (Ike never smoked).The car and trailer started swerving and the cowboys thought they must have a flat. The still-smoldering cigarette had landed back in the wooden slat horse trailer where it caught the straw on the floor of the trailer on fire. By the time Ike looked back in his rear mirror, the flames were leaping up to the top of the open-topped trailer. Ike slammed on his brakes. In a frenzy he freed the horse and got the flames put out, but not before Baldy had received first-degree burns on his left leg from hoof to shoulder and also his left eye. "God a' mighty," Ike sobbed, "we gotta find us a vet!" Ike managed to get him to the nearest veterinarian he could find and was advised to have the horse euthanized and put out of his misery. But Ike did not have the heart to do that. He had heard of a good veterinarian that lived in Utica, Nebraska. Amazingly enough, they were able to coax Baldy back into the trailer—likely heavily sedated by the vet—and they went on to Burwell. As luck would have it, that veterinarian, Dr. Darrel S. Trump, happened to be there, visiting the rodeo. When Ike had him look at Baldy, he told Ike he thought he could save the horse but it was going to take a long process and Ike would have to leave him with him for several months. Ike was ready to do anything humanly possible to save his beloved roping horse.

Dr. Trump took the horse back with him to his clinic in Utica. He grafted chicken skin onto Baldy's badly burned leg, and put several different oils and salves on his burns. He kept him in a screened stall to keep flies away from his open wounds, and rode him fifteen miles each day in the sand hills of Nebraska to build his muscles back. The muscles had not been damaged from the fire but he needed his strength built back up during this long confinement. Baldy's eye was even saved by the capable and dedicated veterinarian.

In April 1938, a little over eight months after Ike left him, he returned to pick him up. The horse would remain badly scarred for the rest of his life, but Dr. Trump had saved him. After the horse's terrible experience he was not trailer shy, which was probably due to the excellent handling he got. Many cowboys told Ike that even if the veterinarian could save the horse, he would be ruined for roping. Not so, in Ike's mind, as he had faith in Ol' Baldy. He kept telling them that he would come back and be a better horse than before, that he "will burn a hole in your pocket—he will stop so hard," as Ike would put it, and he did just that!

Ike with Baldy and Trombone (Ace Soward's horse) in the trailer, 1937.

Baldy recovered and went on to become the most celebrated rodeo horse, specializing in calf-roping, in the history of the sport. In his lifetime career, with men like Rude, Troy Fort, Clyde and Jiggs Burk, Cotton Lee, and Jack Skipworth in the saddle, it has been estimated that Baldy won over $300,000.[5]

If you ask any of the old, seasoned calf ropers throughout the country, "Who was the greatest calf horse of all time?" Chances are the reply will be, "Baldy." During the 1930s, '40s, and early '50s, more than $300,000 was won off Baldy in Rodeo Cowboys Association rodeos. During those years this was a very large sum of money. Several World Calf Roping titles were won off Baldy by the few cowboys who could endure his bone-jarring stop. In calf roping competition, a horse that stops abruptly after the cowboy has roped the calf is considered a good roping horse. This highly desired trait allows the cowboy to quickly dismount, run down the rope, and tie the calf in the shortest time possible.

After his burn healed, the horse came back and it was reported from various articles and even by Ike that his famous "stop" was even better, and he was an even harder horse for many ropers to ride because of it. He would just eject them right over his head if they weren't dismounting at the critical time. Ike and a few others mentioned above were the select few who could ride the horse through his "stop."

Ike wrote of Baldy's winnings in a letter to a friend:

> In 1937 Jess Goodspeed was roping on him at Rocky Ford, Colorado. He won both first day monies there. One calf tied in 10.6 and one in 13. These were bald faced calves following their mammys. From there we came to Oklahoma City and I won all three first day monies, the longest I was on a calf was 14.2. As far as his biggest shows, we made them all: Madison Square Garden, Pendleton, Oregon, Cheyenne, Wyoming, Salinas, California, Ft. Worth, Texas, Calgary, Canada, and all the rest.

Everett Bowman, who was in 1936 the first president of the Cowboys Turtle Association, once said of Baldy, "He must have a heart as big as a wash tub." The horse also picked up a nickname: "the Scar Legged Sorrel."

Seven months after Ike got Baldy back, he also had his new bride, Cleo, with him. They proceeded on their journey of crisscrossing the United States and into Canada, traveling the rodeo circuit for the next five years. They traveled to Calgary, Canada; Baton Rouge, Louisiana; New York City, New York; Chicago, Illinois; Little Rock, Arkansas; Oklahoma City, Woodward, and Vinita, Oklahoma; Clovis, New Mexico; Pittsburg, Pennsylvania; Fort Worth and Houston, Texas; Cleveland, Ohio; Colorado Springs, Colorado; Cheyenne, Wyoming; and Elko and Winnemucca, Nevada, to name a few among many. Cleo learned to pull the horse trailer and was a big help in driving. When the couple would arrive at a rodeo, Cleo would load up some of the other cowboys' wives to take them on a sight-seeing tour of whatever city they were staying in. Many of the women were reluctant to drive in large cities, but not Cleo. Ike always encouraged Cleo to enjoy life and go see the sights. One city that Cleo never drove in was New York City during the Madison Square Garden rodeo, as, once they arrived there, the car and trailer were parked in a designated storage parking place until the rodeo was over. But that didn't stop Cleo from going on tours and seeing all that New York City had to offer.

At the 1939 Treasure Island Rodeo in San Francisco, California, the cowboys were expected to ride in a parade down the fair's midway to help advertise and promote the rodeo. Contestants were required to ride in parades and in the grand entries at most rodeos during this period, but riding in parades is not something cowboys like to do. Some of the wives got together and asked if they could ride their husband's roping horses in the parade rather than the cowboys. The rodeo committee granted their request, and Cleo and the others had a great time doing this.

Another time at a rodeo in Sidney, Iowa, Andy Jauregui, a prominent stock contractor and rodeo producer who was also quite a good roper

Baldy and his scarred leg. This picture was given to each subscriber of the magazine *Hoof & Horns* for several years.

himself and was one of Ike's many good friends, needed transportation to get his roping horse to a rodeo at Palm Springs, California. Ike had often team roped with Andy. Ike was attending another rodeo, but had planned to catch a ride with a friend to get to Palm Springs, where Cleo would meet him, having hauled Baldy there by herself. Ike told Andy that Cleo could bring his horse also. Back then not too many women would pull horse trailers so Andy was reluctant, but Ike convinced him that Cleo had lots of driving hours of practice of pulling a horse trailer, so Andy gave in. By the time the two cowboys arrived at Palm Springs, Cleo had the horses already in a stall awaiting them. Ike never learned to back a trailer. He always let Cleo do that, as well as a good amount of the driving.

In 1939, with Ike riding Baldy, he won the calf-roping again at Calgary, Canada, and an engraved wristwatch. Ike was forty-five years old. This is believed to be a record for the oldest cowboy to have ever won the calf-roping at Calgary.

The very next year, 1940, Ike won the J. O. Selman Trophy at Woodward, Oklahoma, given to the best all-around cowboy who won the most money in any two contested events over the duration of the rodeo at Woodward. Ike won for his accumulation of points in both calf roping (on Baldy) and

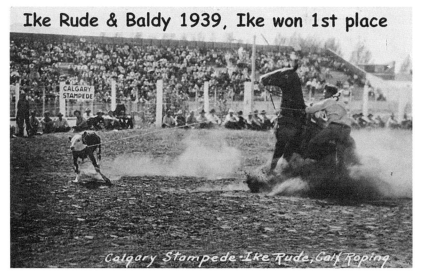

Ike roping on Baldy at Calgary, Canada, where he won the calf roping, 1939. Photo courtesy of the Old Greer County Museum and Hall of Fame, Mangum, Oklahoma.

steer roping (on Bullet). A newspaper article said that during the three-day rodeo there was a crowd of 35,000 total, with 13,000 spectators attending the last performance.

Ike was winning regularly in steer roping. He was still roping on Bullet, and as told in chapter 10, Ike won World Champion Steer Roper on him in 1941, making this his first "official" world championship title. He also had won the steer roping at Cheyenne, Wyoming, that year.

Other cowboys who rode Ike's horses were also winning. Ike mounted many cowboys on Baldy at the rodeos for a percentage of their winnings. Baldy was a most sought-after horse to compete on. Jack Skipworth, Everett Shaw, Buckshot Sorrells, Cotton Lee, Clyde Burke, Troy Fort, and Toots Mansfield were among the few cowboys who were successful in roping off him.

Then in 1942 things changed . . . Cleo was pregnant with their first child. Ike, of course, had never saved any of his winnings, so he needed to make some money. Up until this time, it was easy come and easy go for Ike. Making money was no problem; just having plenty to get to the next roping and pay living expenses for him and Cleo was all Ike desired. But now Ike was forty-eight years old, and the younger cowboys were starting to win in calf roping. He was still winning regularly in steer roping, but steer roping did not pay as well as calf roping as there weren't that many rodeos that held that event. In 1942 at Denver, during the National Western Stock Show and Rodeo, Ike had just won the first go-round in calf roping. He was celebrating his win when Clyde Burke approached him to buy Baldy. That night Ike had spouted off that it would take $2,500 to buy a horse like Baldy, never dreaming that Clyde, or anyone else, could or would pay that kind of money for a roping horse. This was only a few years after people were recovering from the Great Depression and money was hard for anyone to come by, let alone for a rodeo cowboy to be able to meet that price! But the next morning, Clyde came to Ike with the money. With tears in his eyes, Ike handed the lead rope to Clyde, and his beloved horse was gone. Ike would not back down from his word even though it was a struggle for him not to. The next go-round with his new horse, Clyde won first. Many times after that, Ike said it was the worst mistake he ever made in his life to have priced Baldy. Newspapers all over the country printed the event for being the highest price ever paid for a roping horse. In today's times, that would be nothing, but back then it was an unheard-of price for a roping horse.

Clyde owned Baldy until 1945, when Clyde was killed at the Denver rodeo while he was hazing for a friend in the steer wrestling using another horse. His widow sold Baldy to Troy Fort of Lovington, New Mexico, where Baldy remained until the famous horse's death in 1961. Baldy is buried at the Jake McClure Arena at Lovington, New Mexico, where a monument is erected in the horse's memory.

The famous rope horse was inducted into the ProRodeo Cowboy Hall of Fame in Colorado Springs, Colorado, in 1979. A bronze and aggregate stone monument to him is also displayed at the National Cowboy and Western Heritage Museum in Oklahoma City in its outdoor garden. While visiting the International Museum of the Horse at Lexington, Kentucky, in the late 1990s, I found a plaque hanging on the museum's walls commemorating Baldy as the "Greatest Roping Horse of All Time," along with Ike Rude's credit for training and owning him.

TWELVE

Early-Day Family Life on the Road, 1942–1946

For five years the couple had traveled from one rodeo to another. Then on October 4, 1942, a son was born to Ike and Cleo Rude. They named him Billy Ike Rude. The couple had been renting a small acreage at Pawhuska, Oklahoma, where they lived between travels. They had discussed buying a small ranch there, but in the end Ike's free spirit won out, convincing him that it would carry with it too many responsibilities that would keep him from roping. So they never owned a home until decades later.

After selling Baldy, Ike had a calf horse he called Chamico for a short time in 1942.

In 1943 Ike purchased a horse that was a half-brother to Bullet and named him Joe. Ike trained him for steer roping. At Cheyenne Frontier Days, Ike let Buckshot Sorrells use him to trip steers, with Buckshot winning the average on Joe. The only other information that was obtained regarding Joe was that he had gotten in some wire shortly after the rodeo at Cheyenne and was cut up so badly that he had to be put down. This was unfortunate, as Joe had the makings of an outstanding roping horse.

Cheyenne was not the first time Buckshot Sorrells had borrowed one of Ike's horses. In fact, he did so often, as he and Ike were the best of friends who had a lot in common: Buckshot was a top calf roper, team roper, and steer wrestler throughout the 1930s. The two would often bunk together while traveling. Ike would often be the hazer for Buckshot in the steer-wrestling event. Only after several years of close friendship and travels did they get around to talking about their heritage. Buckshot told Ike that his mother's last name was Pyeatt and her family had come from Tennessee. Ike thought that was strange, as his mother's maiden name was Pyeatt, and

IKE RUDE, MANGUM, OKLA.,
WORLD FAMOUS CONTEST ROPER

Ike on Chamico, 1942.

her family had come from there also. They came to the conclusion they were first cousins, and all this time they never knew it!

Having a family did not slow down Ike's travels to rodeos in any way. Cleo and baby went with him most of the time, but sometimes Cleo and Bill would stay at Cleo's mother's place in Buffalo. When she did travel to the rodeos with Ike, Cleo would have to stay at the motel frequently with Bill while Ike would go out to the rodeo grounds to exercise his horse and pre-run the cattle for the upcoming roping. This got very old and lonesome for Cleo, staying at the motel for long periods of time, so she had an idea—why didn't they get a tent and just camp out at the rodeo grounds? That way Ike wouldn't have to come back and forth to the motel and Cleo would be at the rodeo grounds where she wouldn't be so lonesome. Also, they wouldn't have to be out the expense of a motel and restaurant. Ike agreed that would be a good idea, so they purchased a camp stove for cooking and a tent. They loved this arrangement. Soon thereafter, other rodeo families started to join them, and for a few years little tent cities were formed at the rodeo grounds, all thanks to Cleo's idea. Members of Indian tribes would often camp at the rodeo grounds with their tepees, as they were still participating in many of the rodeos, performing Indian dances and riding in horse-relay races. Only a few of the rodeos are left that still have the Indian camps. The cowboys would set up camp in their area, and the Indians would do the same in their area. It wasn't long before Cleo had all the company she wanted. Ike would often have to go from tent to tent to find her, as she loved to socialize. The roping families bonded by living like this. It was always fun to find your camping spot at the next rodeo grounds and set up close to friends. Most people would cook their meals at their tents. Cleo's campsite was always very neat and tidy. When the weather was bad, they would get a motel room, or when the rodeo lasted for several days, sometimes they would rent a motel room for one night so they could take a good bath, but often they would just boil water on their camp stove and bathe in a washtub in the tent. Cleo became very adaptable and efficient at setting up the campsite. She much preferred to set up the tent herself as she didn't think Ike stretched it tight enough. These cowboy tent cities were popular until the early 1950s, when a more sophisticated form of camping took over with camper trailers and camper shells on backs of pickups.

Cleo was also much better at backing the horse trailer than Ike, so while she took over this chore, Ike would go tend to his horse and get to practice roping his steer horns tied to a bale of hay or straw, which he did during any free time he had for the majority of his life. Cleo became efficient at much of the vehicle maintenance, or maintenance of any sort, and camping responsibilities, as well as a lot of the driving duties while on the road.

Since steer roping was being outlawed in so many states and they weren't having them as frequently at rodeos as before, then matched ropings between the top steer ropers became popular during this time. The billboards would advertise these matched ropings extensively and they were very well attended by the public. The general public was still very interested in watching this event, especially in the ranching states.

In 1942 Ike and Dick Truitt were matched against one another at a steer roping at Dewey, Oklahoma. The billboards advertised "Dick Truitt from Stonewall, Oklahoma, 1939 Winner of Cheyenne Frontier Days and Ike Rude, from Pawhuska, Oklahoma, 1941 Winner of Cheyenne Frontier Days." They each roped twelve steers. Ike won.

While attending the rodeo at Cheyenne, Wyoming, in 1943, Ike performed an exhibition in roping. A Cheyenne newspaper ran an article that said:

> A steer can be roped from an army jeep, but the four cylinders under the hood of the blitz buggy don't substitute for a good roping horse.
>
> Ike Rude, of Pawhuska, Okla. Roped a loping longhorn from a jeep at the Cheyenne's Frontier Days rodeo today before 11,000 spectators, but when it came to "busting" the animal, the jeep might as well have been in Sicily.
>
> Attempting to circle the steer in order to trip him was too much, and Rude's precious lariat parted.[1]

Also in 1943 Ike again won the steer roping at Pendleton, Oregon. That same year at Woodward, Oklahoma, Ike and Everett Shaw were pitted against each other in a matched roping for an entry fee of $5,000 each. Ike came out the winner.

The year 1943 would be the last one that Ike attended the Madison Square Garden Rodeo in New York City, ending his attendance there from

Ike at Pendleton, Oregon, 1944. Notice the tepees in the background.

the first rodeo they ever had in 1922 through to 1943, and he only missed once during these twenty-one years.

In 1945, Ike was still roping calves at the age of fifty-one when he won the calf roping at El Centro, California. More than likely this is another rodeo where he would be the oldest to ever win the calf roping. However, there are no archives I have found to substantiate this.

Also in 1945, Cleo became pregnant with their second child. The family was staying at Buffalo, Oklahoma, with Cleo's mother in between rodeos. The Ada, Oklahoma, Fireman's Rodeo was coming up about the time Cleo was to deliver their child. Ike wasn't going to go, but Cleo insisted that he go, as he usually made money at Ada in the steer roping. Besides that, she said that her sister Twila could drive her to Woodward to the hospital if the baby came before he got home. That is exactly what happened. A daughter was born and they named me Sammie Kay, after Ike's father, Sam Rude. Ike was at Ada, roping at the rodeo, when he received the telegram, then during the rodeo the announcer told the crowd that Ike Rude had a new daughter! What a baby announcement! That was how I made it into this world.

Soon thereafter, the family of four hit the road again traveling to rodeos. They continued to camp out at the rodeo grounds, or sometimes they would camp out in a nearby pasture belonging to someone Ike knew from his travels.

In 1946, the family rented a small acreage and house at Dodge City, Kansas, and made that their stop-over in between their rodeo travels. In Ike's time at home, he broke horses for Roy Evans, a local rancher.

THIRTEEN

Buster, 1946–1950

I n 1946, Ike's search for his next great horse took him back to Ronald Mason's Cross J Ranch to purchase Buster. Buster's sire was the Thoroughbred Beggar Boy, who was a full brother to Black Gold, winner of the Kentucky Derby in 1924, and his dam was Bay Babe. Both belonged to Mason. Bay Babe's sire was Old Red Buck and her dam was Babe Dawson, raised by John Dawson, who was also the dam of Baldy. Buster was a big, stout, brown, good-looking gelding that stood 15.1 hands, or 5 feet, 1 inch, and weighed around 1,200 pounds. He was a six-year-old ranch horse when Ike purchased him. According to Ronald's son Corbett Mason, Bill Hedge worked there at that time, so more than likely it was Bill who had been doing ranch work with the horse and had trained him up to that point. Years later, Bill created the first pari-mutuel horse racetrack in Oklahoma called Blue Ribbon Downs at Sallisaw, Oklahoma.

Shortly after purchasing the horse, Ike won the 1946 steer roping at Lawton, Oklahoma, and Ozona, Texas, riding Buster. In organized rodeo, steer roping was being frowned upon more and more by the Humane Society. Rodeo committees, which in the past had included steer ropings at their rodeos, were starting to abolish them. So steer roping, as a separate individual event, was being held by ranches and other organizations. A lot of jackpot steer ropings were being held. There would be no money added to the winnings, just the entry fees of all the cowboys were combined in the purse. Matched ropings were organized quite often between the best of the best ropers of that era. As a spectator and gambling sport, it still drew a large crowd of the general public, as it was much wilder and more entertaining than calf or team roping. These events were widely advertised and attended by thousands from miles around. They also had calcuttas at these events. Calcuttas are a bidding auction where people "buy" whichever cowboy they thought would win, both by go-rounds and the average. The

Powder River, An Inch Deep and A Mile Wide!

The WILD BUNCH

Vol. 4, No. 2   RODEO HALL OF FAME, OKLAHOMA CITY, OK   MAY, 1982

IKE RUDE

Mounted on the
Great Steer
Horse Called Buster

(See Page 12)

National Cowboy
Hall of Fame Library

Ike on Buster, 1948. Cover of *The Wild Bunch,* vol. 4, no. 2 (May 1982). Dickinson Research Center, National Cowboy and Western Heritage Museum.

calcutta event usually paid more to the winners than the participating cowboys even received for competing. The calcuttas would draw many professional gamblers and celebrities to bid on the cowboys.

A match between Ike and Carl Arnold, the 1945 World Champion Steer Roper from Buckeye, Arizona, was held at Tucson in 1946. This time each roped twelve Mexican steers for a $10,000 purse. During this event there was also a competition bull ride pitting champion bull rider Dick Griffith against the Speckled Brahma, an unridden bull. Carl defeated Ike at their event. The winner is unknown as to the other event, the bull, or the rider.

At Dewey, Oklahoma, Everett Shaw of Stonewall, Oklahoma, 1944 World Champion Steer Roper, was matched against Ike. Ike defeated Everett. The two would be pitted against each other two more times. The third time, in a match held at San Angelo, Texas, in 1947, Everett defeated Ike.

In 1947, a matched roping between Cotton Lee, 1946 World Champion Steer Roper, and Ike was also held at San Angelo. That year, each roped ten head. The posters read,

> Two of the World's most famous steer ropers that are just as fast and salty as they ever come, roping big, long-horned Mexican steers. Roped, tripped and tied in the open, just as they did fifty years ago. We are prepared for a big crowd from everywhere. Better wire or call for hotel accommodations. The town will be packed.[1]

The phrase "roped, tripped and tied in the open" meant the event was staged out in an open pasture, not in an arena. Ike won this one.

In late 1947, the Ike Rude family relocated their home to Newhall, California. Bill was in the first grade, so they had to stay in one place long enough so he could attend school. Team roping had taken over California and Arizona. But in these early years, team roping had not yet spread across the United States, and many places had never heard of it.

Dally team roping was featured in California. After the header makes the catch, the rope is dallied around the saddle horn to secure the animal, the header then rides away from the steer on the animal's left side and pulls the steer so the heeler can rope his hind legs. After the heeler makes the catch, then he, too, dallies his rope around the saddle horn. The header then turns his horse to face the steer. Both horses must be facing the steer and ropes stretched tight before the time stops for this event.

Arizona offered tie-down team roping, sometimes referred to as "hard and fast" roping. Tie-down team roping originated in the mountains of Arizona, where Ike had worked in his younger years. Both cowboys, the header and heeler, would have their ropes tied to the saddle horn before roping the animal. After the header had roped the steer, he followed the same procedure by riding off to the left side of the steer and pulling him so

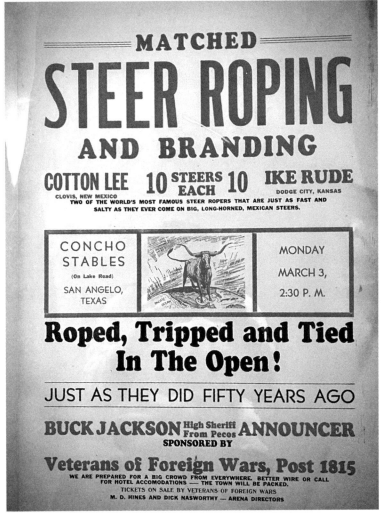

Poster advertising Ike and Cotton Lee's matched roping at San Angelo, Texas, 1947.

Ike, age fifty-two, calf roping on Buster at Lewiston, Idaho, 1946.

Ike steer roping on Buster at Encampment, Wyoming, 1947.

the heeler could make his catch of the hind legs. Upon the heeler catching the legs, he would then turn his horse away from the steer. Both header and heeler would pull on the animal, with their horses facing away from him, in order to stretch him out and pull him down. The header then would get off his horse and run back to further secure the animal by tying his hind legs together with a square knot. Once tied, the cowboy threw his hands in the air to signal for time to stop for this event. This form of team roping was popular throughout Arizona at this time. But by 1970 it was abolished as once again the Humane Society thought it was too rough on livestock.

About every weekend one could go to a rodeo or jackpot somewhere and compete in these two states. Therefore, moving to California seemed to be the best solution for Ike. This way, he was able to rope and keep Bill in school. Then in the summertime, the family would take off and rodeo full-time, being on the road constantly.

They rented a small house about three or four miles from Andy Jaure-gui's home. Andy's ranch was a backdrop for many movie productions. In their front yard was a huge tree that, along with the barn, appeared in many scenes of Western movies in those days. Ike spent a lot of time over at Andy's. The two team roped together on many occasions at the rodeos and jackpots. Andy was also a rodeo stock producer and he himself had won the title of World Champion Steer Roper in 1931 and World Champion Team Roper in 1934.

Ike and Cleo traded their car for a station wagon. They took out the back seat. A wooden frame was built in the back to hold a mattress. This became the family's bedroom while traveling and attending the rodeos. Most of the time, when the weather was nice, Ike preferred to put his bedroll out on the ground and sleep there, just as he had done for so many years while working on the large ranches in his younger days. This gave Mom, Bill, and me more room in the station wagon. Mom had also made modifications inside our two-horse wooden trailer. When we got to our destination, the first thing Mom would do was clean out the horse trailer and set up her kitchen in the manger of the trailer. The manger held all of the cooking utensils and dishes. She would get the camp stove out, set it up, and unlatch the drop-down board she had installed inside the side of the trailer for their dining table, and voilà! Our home was set up and ready for occupancy for the duration of the rodeo. She would also go to the nearest store that sold big chunks of ice, put it in a box, and keep it covered with a tarp in a shaded area. That was our refrigerator.

That year, 1947, roping off Buster, Ike won the steer stopping at Redbluff, California. By then it was outlawed in California to trip steers, so they switched to "steer stopping." He also won in steer roping at the rodeos at Ada, Mangum, and Waurika, Oklahoma. There were, of course, many other winnings and placings throughout Ike's rodeo career, but only the ones for which I have found records are mentioned here.

In 1947 Ike was fifty-three years old. He won his second title as World Champion Steer Roper using Buster and Rock, Jim Snively's good steer roping horse. The next year, on Buster, Ike finished runner-up as the steer roping world champion.

Ike won the first team roping held at Oakdale, California, in 1948 as well as winning the rodeo's all-around title. Oakdale was considered at that time to be the toughest team roping in the world. He also received a gold-and-ruby-studded belt buckle. His partner is unknown, but I am presuming it was the great roping artist from Mexico, Tony Altamirano. Ike roped with Tony again in 1949, placing third. His wins for that year also included the calf roping and steer roping at Meade, Kansas, and the steer roping at Mangum and Ada, Oklahoma. Ike won a jackpot steer roping at Ruidoso and Deming, New Mexico, and placed second at Encampment, Wyoming, in a jackpot. He also placed several times in day moneys in the rodeo steer roping at Rockford, Illinois.

As George Williams wrote:

> Buster wasn't as good a calf horse as Baldy and wasn't as good a steer horse as Bullet. But he was a whale of a horse. Buster was one of the best all-around rope horses that the sport has ever seen. Of a human-like disposition, it was hard to tell who loved roping the most, Ike or Buster. One year in the calf roping at New York's Madison Square Garden rodeo, Ike mounted Homer Pettigrew, Buckshot Sorrells, Shoat Webster, Claude Henson and Everett Shaw on Buster and they made him a "whole sack full of money."[2]

By now, Ike was fifty-four years old. He decided it was time to give up calf-roping, as he said the "younger boys" were starting to win more than he was. But he figured he could keep steer roping and team roping with the best of them, and he did just that. He went back to Madison Square Garden for one last time in 1948, which would end his long career of twenty-five years of attending since its origin.

At the 1948 Lasso del Llano, the big steer roping contest held every Labor Day weekend at Clovis, New Mexico, Ike was dubbed in an article in the *Rodeo Sports News* as the "smallest professional steer buster in the business." Ike had some very bad luck at Clovis. Riding Buster, he had roped and was tripping his first steer when all of a sudden his saddle rigging broke in two and was yanked clean off Buster's back. Ike went flying through the air in one direction and his saddle went the other. Knowing his $1,000 entry fee and his chance of winning the average were gone, Ike picked himself up off the ground and was grinning and waving to the crowd as he walked back to the chutes. The arena director had captured Buster. Neither was injured. This was one of many wrecks that Ike had endured in his life without ever seeming to be injured. However, Ike swore he would never again ride any other saddle than a Hamley, a prominent saddle maker at Pendleton, Oregon.

Ike standing with Buster at Rockford, Illinois, 1948.

Ike steer roping on Buster at Crystal Lake, South Dakota, 1949. Notice Buster is holding his front foot up, indicating his unsoundness due to ring bone.

Ike was doing his fair share of winning in team roping on Buster. Once, a California roper offered Ike $6,000 to buy the horse, but Ike wouldn't sell. In the late 1940s, this was a lot of money to be offered for a rope horse. Ike's reply was, "Why would I want to sell him? He is good in all three roping events." He had already made this mistake once in his life by pricing Baldy and thinking no one would pay that for a horse. He never wanted to make that same mistake again!

According to Willard Porter, "The last steer roping in which Ike roped on Buster was at Lander, Wyoming in 1950. After this event Buster was diagnosed with ring bone, which is an unsoundness in a horses' legs."[3] He had to be destroyed. Ike could not bear to do this himself, as he loved the horse so much. Ace Soward, Ike's brother-in-law, told Ike he would take care of it for him. Ike left his beloved companion at Buffalo, Oklahoma, where Ace lived, and Ike and his family drove back to their home in Newhall, without Buster.

Although Buster never was so honored in halls of fame as were Baldy and Bullet, he was another of Ike's great and famous horses. Willard Porter wrote in his book *13 Flat*, "Buster was one of the best all-around rope horses—steer busting, team tying, and calf roping—in the sport's history."[4]

RECOLLECTIONS

Bill and I have such unique and fond memories of growing up as a "traveling rodeo family." It just seemed so normal to us at that time in our young years. Little did we know it was anything but normal. Dad was always so entertaining to be around. He was a great singer and usually would sing old cowboy songs or old hymns he remembered from attending church with his mother during his childhood. He also would recite cowboy poetry he had learned on the ranches in his chuck wagon days. We kids would urge him to sing, and, usually, when he would get behind the wheel to drive, he would sing for hours. He really was very, very good. One of my favorites, I do remember, was "The Strawberry Roan." He would recite many cowboy poems like "Hell on the Mountainside," and so many more. "The Sierry Petes" was one of his, and our, favorites. "Sierry Petes" is a colloquial pronunciation by Gail Gardner, the cowboy poet who wrote the poem. This refers to a mountain range west of Prescott, Arizona, called the "Sierra Prieta." The following is Ike's version of the poem, the way Bill and I remember him reciting it:

The Sierry Petes
By Gail Gardner, 1917

Away up high in the Sierry Petes,
Where the yeller pines grow tall,
Ol'e Sandy Bob an' Buster Jiggs
Had a round-up camp last fall.

Oh, they took their horses and branding irons
And maybe a dog or two,
And they 'lowed they'd brand ever long-eared calf
That came into their view.

Now many a long-eared doggie
That didn't bush up by day
Got his long ears whittled and his old hide sizzled
In a most artistic way.

Chapter 13

Now one fine day says Sandy Bob,
As he lays his seagrass down,
"I'm tired of this cow geography,
And I believe I'll go to town."

So they saddles up, and hits a lope,
For it warn't no sight of a ride,
And them were the days that a good cowboy
Could oil up his insides.

They started in at Kaintucky Bar,
At the head of Whiskey Row,
And they winds 'er up at the Depot House,
Some forty drinks below.

They then sets up and turns around,
And they headed the other way,
An' to tell you the honest to goodness truth,
Th em boys got drunk that day.

They was on their way, headed back to camp,
A-packin' a pretty good load,
When who should they meet but the Devil himself,
Come a-prancin' down the road.

Sez he, "You onery cowboy skunks,
You'd better hunt yer holes,
For I've come up from Hell's Rim Rock,
To gather in your souls."

Sez Sandy Bob, "Old Devil be damn,
We boys are kinda tight;
But you ain't a-goin' gather no cowboy souls,
Without one hell of a fight."

So Sandy Bob poked a hole in his rope,
And he swang 'er straight and true.
He lapped it on the Devil's horns,
And he takes his dallies too.

Now Buster Jiggs was a riata man,
With his cat-gut coiled up neat,
So he shakes it out and he built him a loop,
And he roped the Devil's hind feet.

Oh, they stretched him out and they tailed him down,
While the irons was a-gettin' real hot,
They cropped and swaller-forked his ears,
And they branded him up a lot.

They pruned his horns with a dehorning saw,
An' they knotted his tail for a joke,
They rode off and left him there,
Tied up to a Black-Jack oak.

If you're ever up in the Sierry Petes,
An' you hear a mighty wail,
You'll know it's the Devil a-bellerin' around,
By the knots that's in his tail.⁵

One old-time religious song was one of Ike's favorites: "Farther Along." I so wish I could remember them all, but the years have wiped them from my memory. Other kids grew up being recited nursery rhymes, but Bill and I grew up hearing poems and songs of old cowboy life in days gone by. Dad would sometimes throw in a little ditty to the songs that would make us all laugh.

One evening our family was eating supper at Newhall when Dad's friend and our neighbor who lived a little over a half-mile away, Fox O'Callahan, knocked on our door. Fox, who had been a saddle bronc rider and was now a movie actor and stuntman, said he had a call from someone who wanted to talk to Dad. Fox had a telephone; we didn't. Dad told Fox to take a message from whoever it was and he would call them back. Fox said, "No Ike, he wants to talk to you now. The caller said he would hold the line while I came over and got you." Dad finally got up from the supper table and went with Fox, back to his house to take the call. He didn't know what on earth, or who it was, that was so important that it couldn't wait for him to eat his supper. It was Gene Autry on the other end of the phone. He wanted Ike to come to his recording studio in Los Angeles and record some songs. Dad came back home to finish his supper. Mom asked him who it was and what he wanted. When Dad told Mom, she asked, "Well what did you tell him?" Dad's reply was that he told Gene he was not a singer, he was a cowboy, and hung up the phone!

Dad seemed to almost always be in a good mood and having fun. He was almost like a kid himself and was fun to be around. I think this was a quality that came from loving life and loving what he was doing.

His high spirits often inspired the antics of us kids. During a rodeo when Bill was about six and I was around three, we decided we wanted to make some money, so we came up with the idea that we could go around to the other tents in the rodeo camp and charge a penny to come in and serenade the cowboys and families. Bill had a small ukulele that he didn't know how to play, but he would strum on it. We sang "Back in the Saddle Again," a Gene Autry tune. Then, when we got through singing, we would tell the people that they had to pay us another penny for us to leave! We thought we were really clever and raking in the dough. We also liked to collect Coca-cola bottles that were discarded under the bleachers and grandstands because in those days the concession stands would pay you two cents for returning an empty Coke bottle. That was fun and gave us something to do while making us some spending money for bubble gum and candy at the rodeo. It was also so much fun to explore our new "home" at each new rodeo.

When I was about two, we got a pet dog, a Belgian sheepdog. Mom's sister Opal Reger had been breeding and raising them. We named him Napo. Napo went to all the rodeos with us. About a year after we got him, we were traveling from Miles City, Montana, to Twin Falls, Idaho. Dad had made a box for Napo to ride in back in the horse trailer, next to Buster. At that time we just had a two-door car without enough room for Napo to ride in the car with us. We had been traveling all night across Montana, and when we stopped the next morning, we discovered that somehow Napo had gotten out of the box and apparently jumped out of the trailer. He was gone! Dad turned around and drove back down the highway we had just traveled. For three days we went looking for him across Montana. Dad would stop in gas stations, stop highway patrol cars, and anyone else he came across, asking if they had seen a black dog. A few times someone said they had seen a black dog trotting down the highway heading in the

Bill and Sammie at Pendleton, Oregon, 1948.

direction we had initially been traveling when we lost him, but we never caught sight of him. It looked like Napo was lost forever and we had to get on to Twin Falls to make it to the rodeo. So we headed back.

As luck, or fate, would have it, us kids needed a pit stop there on the wide-open Montana highway. When we stopped, Dad noticed a house that sat quite far back from the highway. On the front porch he could just make out the shape of a black dog. On impulse he called out "Napo!" and when he did, the dog perked up his ears, and on the second call it came running pell-mell down the lane to meet us. It was Napo! Dad went to the house and talked to the man there. He told Dad that the day before he had found Napo trotting down the road and could tell the dog was in need of food and water and about worn out, so he encouraged him to his house, where he fed and watered him. Dad tried to pay the man for taking care of Napo, but the man would not take a thing. We were so glad to have our beloved dog back with us. Imagine scouring the Montana highways for a lost dog for three days—and actually finding him!

Mom never had to worry about us kids if Napo was with us. When we lived at Newhall, Dad had rigged up a swing for us with his old lariat ropes and hung it from a tree limb. I was three years old and was swinging in it, but it came time for me to quit and let Bill have his turn, except I didn't want to quit. When Dad came over to get me out of the swing, I yelled, "Get him, Nap!" That dog took into Daddy and he immediately turned me loose. I remember Dad was laughing so hard, as he had no idea that Napo would turn on him to guard us kids like he did. He was a member of our family and a wonderful protector of us kids.

While our family was at the Pinedale, Wyoming, rodeo in 1948, Dad was trying out a couple of new horses. Bill, who was six years old, wanted to go out with Dad to the roping arena while Mom and I stayed at our campgrounds. When Dad let Bill ride one of his horses that he had purchased, Bill got bucked off. He was skinned up fairly bad. We didn't have a kid horse of our own to ride until years later, as we traveled so much and never had our own place to keep one. If Bill or I wanted to ride, we rode Dad's rope horses. Bill could rope dummy steer horns attached to a bale of hay really good as a young boy. In fact, he was so good that Everett Shaw and Clark McEntire (Reba McEntire's father) would come over to our campsite and get into roping contests with Bill, and often Bill could do his share of winning. Clark used to eat with us a lot at our campsite.

When I was about four or five, we were at the yearly Clovis, New Mexico, jackpot steer roping, where it looked like Dad was going to win the average and some big money. Bill and I had the Sears and Roebuck catalog out and we were going through it, plotting and trying to decide on all the new toys we could purchase with Dad's winnings. Well, as can happen, on the last steer roped, Dad went out of his chances to win any money in the average, and the average was where all the jackpot money was paid and distributed to the cowboys. We were heartbroken and Mom was wondering how we were even going to have enough money to get back to California, when Dad rode up with $5,000! Bing Crosby, the famous singer and movie actor, was there, and he had "bought" Dad in the calcutta auction. Because Dad had placed at the top in all but the last go-round, Dad had won Bing a lot of money that day. The calcutta paid on the go-rounds as well as the average, but the roping only paid on who won the average. Bing had graciously given Dad $5,000 out of his winnings because he felt bad for Dad's hard luck on his last steer. Bing was a big fan who liked to gamble. He attended a lot of ropings and several places in California that had calcuttas so he could bet on the cowboys.

When I was somewhere around six years old, I remember being at Gene Autry's ranch in Oklahoma to look at his horses he had raised. Gene wanted to give Dad one from his breeding stock for him to train as a roping horse. If I remember correctly, this was after Buster had to be put down, so Gene probably knew that Dad was out looking for another good replacement and hadn't found one yet. Gene always thought a lot of Dad, even though he had turned him down to be a singer and wouldn't come to his recording studio in Hollywood. Dad left without one because he didn't like the quality of the horses. At a young age I thought, "How could you turn down a horse that Gene Autry wanted to give you?" But Dad knew his horses and how to pick them, and he did not want to put his time in on training one unless it was of his caliber of horseflesh.

Without a Good Horse, 1950–1951

After Buster had to be put down, Ike had a few horses that he trained and competed on in roping events. But for about a year and a half, he did not have one that was of the caliber he was searching for and wanted to own. This did not slow him down from rodeoing though, as cowboys frequently would borrow each other's horse to rope from. All of Ike's life, to this point, he had mounted many cowboys on his horses, and now Ike would rope off of other's horses for the next two years. In 1951, Ike borrowed Rock, Jim Snively's horse, a lot. Some of the places he roped off Rock were at Cheyenne and Laramie, Wyoming, Woodward and Waynoka, Oklahoma, and also at a steer roping contest held at Artesia, New Mexico.

In 1950, our family moved from Newhall to Brawley, California, when I was five years old and starting kindergarten and Bill was in the third grade. While there, Ike worked for the Kalins, who ran some cattle on the sugar beet fields after the harvest, as was being done in the Imperial Valley at that time. Ike could still go to a lot of jackpot team ropings that were held close by Brawley, but come summertime, the Rudes would once again hit the road to attend the steer and team ropings and rodeos around the United States.

During this time, Ike had trouble getting regular access to roping cattle with which he could train a roping horse, so he improvised. He would buy a goat or two, load the goats and the horse up in the trailer, and head for the open desert nearby. He would have Cleo hold the goat until he told her to turn him loose, then Ike, on horseback, would chase the goat across the wide-open desert and rope him. Bill and I would take our toys out to play in the desert while this was taking place.

After the summer rodeo season in 1951, Ike found work at Calipatria, California, with a farmer-rancher who ran cattle on the fields there. Once

Ike steer roping on Rock, Jim Snively's horse, at Waynoka, Oklahoma, 1951.

again, Ike had to settle down for the school season so I could attend first grade and Bill the fourth grade. On one occasion, the man Ike was working for needed to move a large herd of cattle to a different field a few miles away. He felt he needed to hire a few cowboys to help. He told Ike to meet him at the field and he would be there with the cowboys. But when Ike went to meet him and no one showed up, Ike went back to the house and got Cleo, Bill, me, and Napo, the dog, and we moved the cattle. When we finished, we then went back home. Shortly after, the boss man came driving up in his pickup, screeching to a halt at our house. He was frantic, ranting at Ike that somebody had stolen all his cattle. Ike informed him that he, his family, and dog had already moved the cattle. The boss was thunderstruck, unable to believe that one man, his wife, two little kids, and a dog could have moved that many cattle.

Ike's talents were recognized far and wide and in many ways. Rancher Leroy Campbell from Claude, Texas, had raised a Quarter Horse stallion to be the sire of his mare herd. He named the bay horse Ike Rude; his American Quarter Horse Association registration number was P-17290. He stood the horse at stud for many years, and the horse produced a lot of very nice ranch and roping horses around the Texas Panhandle, New Mexico, and Oklahoma throughout the 1950s and '60s.

Bill, Ike, Sammie, and Napo the dog at Brawley, California, 1950.

RECOLLECTIONS

By 1950, a lot of the other cowboy families had started staying in motels or putting campers on the back of their pickups to sleep in, and the tent cities that mom had originated were starting to disappear. By this time, we had also gotten a pickup and had a friend of Dad's build a homemade camper on it. We still used our horse trailer for the kitchen and usually camped out at the rodeo grounds or a pasture somewhere, same as before.

The summer of 1951 Ike got a job working on a ranch in the middle of nowhere in New Mexico. The closest school was Dunlap. There was a small post office and another one-room building there that doubled as the church and school. Dunlap was on New Mexico State Road 20, thirty-four miles southwest of Fort Sumner and fifty miles north of Roswell. It is today a ghost town. Bill and I thought it was the most desolate place we had ever seen. Our house, which was provided for us by the ranch, was a very old adobe house that had no indoor plumbing. There were four rooms. It had two rooms on one side, the living room and kitchen, and two bedrooms on the other side. One had to go outside in order to access the two bedrooms. There were rattlesnakes everywhere! The first week we were there, a rattler bit one of the ranch hands. Before Dad could get the man to the nearest hospital, in Roswell, the man's arm had swollen badly and he was starting to pass out. Dad had to cut the bite with his pocket knife so it would bleed. If I remember correctly, the guy did survive.

The following week, Dad, Mom, Bill, Napo, and I moved a large herd of cattle on horseback. In doing so, we had to herd them across the Pecos River, which at the time the water was up past our stirrups. It was pretty exciting for me as I was only six years old. A few days after that, Dad got up before daylight, as he always did, and went to get his horse out of the corral to saddle him. When he reached up to open the gate, he put his hand on a big ole rattlesnake that was curled up on the post. He came straight back to the house and told Mom to pack up, we were leaving. It was no place to raise a family. We headed back out to California so Dad could search for work.

FIFTEEN

Terrapin, 1951–1956

I n the fall of 1951, a farmer by the name of Roy Sewell from Pampa, Texas, had acquired a big bay, stout, good-looking Quarter Horse that he had been running on the local race tracks. The horse stood about 15.2 hands, or 5 feet, 2 inches, and weighed an impressive 1,300 pounds! His sire was Cowpuncher, who was by Midnight, and his dam was Pope's Goldie by Yellow Boy. It had beaten every horse in the Texas Panhandle and Roy was no longer able to get others to match a race against the horse because of his record of wins. Roy had no desire to travel to races far away, as his means of making a living was his farm. It was not feasible for him to be gone for extended periods of time. The horse, named Terrapin, had already made him a lot of money from his local winnings. As Roy had always been a big fan of Ike's and had followed his career and watched him rope at some of the local rodeos, he knew Ike had lost Buster a few years prior and was still in search of a good horse. Roy contacted Ike to tell him he wanted to give Terrapin to Ike to make a steer roping horse. On the way to trying out the ranch job at Dunlap, New Mexico, Ike took us to Mr. Sewell's farm to look at the horse. Not really expecting much, but as a courtesy to Mr. Sewell for the generous offer, we made the stop. What Ike saw was one of the best-looking and stoutest geldings he had ever seen in his life. Immediately Ike knew he had to have him. Out of gratitude, Ike insisted he pay $500 for him.

After the short few weeks on the Dunlap, New Mexico, ranch, Ike once again loaded up and headed back to California to look for work during the school season. He landed a job at Orita Land and Cattle Company, at Brawley. Orita was the biggest feed-lot operation of that time. Ed Rutherford, the owner and Ike's boss, knew of Ike and his roping abilities. When he hired Ike, Mr. Rutherford agreed that Ike could take off and rodeo during the summer months. He also would be able to take off to go to some of the local rodeos and ropings that were held during the winter. Bill and I attended a three-room country school. First and second grades were in one room; third, fourth, and fifth in another; and sixth, seventh, and eighth in another. It was a wonderful country school. Both of us kids happily attended there for the next seven years. Ike's job was to take care of about 1,900 head of cattle that were out in the fields before they came in to the feed lot to be fattened up and sold for butchering. Ike was able to do a lot of roping practice, as they would rope the cows to doctor them in the fields. Any time they had to load or count cattle in the feed lot, Ed

Ike Rude, who has enjoyed a long career as a professional cowboy, has also enjoyed a long record of winning honors. He made only 26 professional appearances at the old Madison Square Garden in New York City.
When asked about his family's participation in related sports, he says they went along on his trips!

Ike Rude-Age 61
On Tarpin-Yuma Ariz.
1955

Ike on Terrapin, 1953.

always called on Ike to help out with that. Ike could count cattle quicker than anyone he ever saw. He could count by twos, threes, however they went past him. Ike was great at doing math in his head. Of course by this time Ike had plenty of experience of counting cattle from his old ranch working days. At fifty-eight years old, Ike had the kind of experience the younger cowboys that he worked with could only imagine.

Ike wrote to Roy Sewell about his excitement with his new rope horse: "Terrapin is sure a good horse. He is just exactly what I wanted. He will make the boys' eyes stick out when they see him." Stick out they did, as in the year 1953 Ike—at the age of fifty-nine—won his third World Champion Steer Roping title, on Terrapin. That year he won or placed at Cheyenne and Pinedale, Wyoming; Pendleton, Oregon; and Vinita, Woodward, and McAlester, Oklahoma.

For thirty-seven years Ike had the honor of being the oldest cowboy to ever win a World Championship title in the ProRodeo Cowboys Association. For several years in the 1950s and '60s, every time a pair of Wrangler jeans was purchased, in the hip pocket would be a little pamphlet of statics of rodeo cowboys. Listed in it was Ike Rude's name for having been the oldest cowboy to ever win a World Championship. In 2016, Mary Burger won the World Championship in women's barrel racing at sixty-eight years old, which topped Ike's record. But it remains that Ike is still the oldest cow*boy* to have ever won such a title.

Many rodeo announcers had fun with Ike, commenting on such a little man on a big horse. They would announce, "Folks, it is worth the price of admission just to watch this little guy get on this big horse." Ike was always one of the announcers' favorite contestants to work with. As anyone could tell, Ike was having fun when he came out of the roping chute. He would usually let out a big war whoop and have a huge grin on his face. Before the rodeos would begin, often Ike would be found behind the bucking chutes entertaining the cowboys with his stories and antics or poems and songs of his old cowpunching days in the early 1900s. Casey Tibbs, a most prominent and colorful bronc rider in the 1950s and '60s, was one of many who always sought Ike out at the rodeos. Casey would get Ike to come over and tell stories to his bronc-riding buddies. Ike was a true cowboy character. Ike also liked to shoot craps with the other cowboys while they were waiting for the rodeo to start.

Ike attended about every rodeo and roping that he could possibly get to for many, many years. As mentioned before, Ike had no responsibilities

Ike steer roping on Terrapin at Yuma, Arizona, 1955.

or home to have to go back to until us kids started attending school. That freedom put him in a unique position compared to about every cowboy I can think of who competed in the roping events, as they all had a ranch or job that needed attended.

The *Denver Post* newspaper loved to write articles about Ike during the Cheyenne Frontier Days rodeo. Once an interviewer asked which he would rather be: president of the United States or World Champion roper? Ike's answer was an indignant, quick, "Hell, he can't rope!"

In 1953, at a Quarter Horse show held at Buffalo, Oklahoma, eleven-year-old Bill wanted to show Terrapin in the Aged Gelding Halter class. Buffalo always held a large annual Quarter Horse show and contestants came from many states to compete. Terrapin was named Grand Champion Gelding. The following year, at aged nine, I won the honors with him again. These were the only times the horse was ever showed at an American Quarter Horse show and was grand champion both times. Terrapin was a proven, hard-to-beat race horse, a grand champion halter horse, and also a world-class steer roping horse. He had carried Ike to his final World Champion Steer Roping title.

Ike team roping (heading) on Terrapin at Ventura, California, 1955.

While living at Brawley during the winter months, Ike would always make the rodeo that was held at Yuma, Arizona. Yuma is only seventy miles southeast of Brawley. To get there the family would have to cross the Algodones Sand Dunes. Our route took us near the old wooden plank road that was built in 1915 as a commercial route between San Diego and Yuma. Ike would tell us that in the early mid-1920s, he traveled that road by car with his traveling partners, pulling a horse trailer. The remainder of a one-lane wooden plank road that was still partially visible from the paved road stretched a total of six-and-a-half miles across the sand dunes. Ike said that if you met a vehicle coming from the opposite direction, one of the vehicles would have to back up to get to a double-width section of wood planks to pull over so that the other vehicle could pass. These double sections were placed at intervals, perhaps about every quarter- or half-mile, for passing purposes.

In 1956, Ike was sixty-two years old. At this age, most rodeo cowboys had retired. Team ropers could keep roping at an older age, as it wasn't as physically demanding. But steer roping is a very physical roping event, requiring a cowboy to rope, trip, dismount at a high rate of speed, and tie the steer. And yet, Ike won the Cheyenne Frontier Days that year! He won a silver belt buckle with diamonds and a saddle, the latter of which is on display at the National Cowboy and Western Heritage Museum's American Rodeo Gallery in Oklahoma City along with other trophies he

Ike, sixty-one years old, at Cheyenne Frontier Days, 1955.

won throughout his career. He is, to date, the oldest cowboy to have ever won the steer roping at Cheyenne. It will be a hard record to beat!

Sadly, 1956 was the last year that Ike would get to rope off of Terrapin, as the horse became lame. He was diagnosed with a broken bone in his foot and had to be put down.

RECOLLECTIONS

Bill, by this time, had taken an interest in baseball. Unfortunately, he never was able to have a horse of his own to learn to rope on or access to cattle where he could practice, so he gradually took his interests to a different area. I remember Dad always supported him. When Dad would come home from work in the evenings, usually he would pitch balls to Bill for him to practice catching and batting. I, however, had a huge interest in horses and wanted to run barrels. I joined a 4-H horse group during this time and started competing in horse shows.

Because Bill wanted to join a little league baseball team after school was out, we left California for Buffalo, Oklahoma, where our grandmother lived. Dad would drop Bill, Mom, and me off there for the summer while he made the rodeo circuit. Then, as school was beginning to start, he would pick us up. Usually we would all go to Pendleton, Oregon, to the rodeo, then on down to the team roping at Oakdale, California. We were usually about two weeks late getting back to Brawley after school had started. The country schoolteachers were always accommodating in letting us make up the schoolwork we had missed.

From the time both Bill and I can remember, we would be awakened every morning by the sound of Dad's lariat slapping on a set of dummy steer horns tied to a wooden sawhorse. When he practiced his roping, he always tried to rope them at least one hundred times before he went to work to take care of the cattle. In California's Imperial Valley, where we lived at this time, it would get so hot during the day that ranch and cow work needed to be done by noon. Dad would get up around 4:00 in the morning to practice, and turn on the porch light or headlights on the car if we were on the road somewhere.

When we were traveling, us kids always wanted Mom to drive, as Dad would drive too slowly, about forty-five miles per hour! This was before the interstate highways and most all roads were two lanes. I think fifty-five or sixty was the usual speed limit, and Mom would drive closer to that. It always amazed us kids that Dad could calculate the time we would get to the next town without a map. He had traveled the United States from end to end so many times that he knew many of the towns and how many miles it was between them. It was like traveling with a GPS many years before it was invented!

When traveling over a mountain range, it was not unusual for cars or pickups to overheat if they were pulling a load. Many times, I remember, we would unload the horses at the bottom, then Dad and I would ride them to the top of the mountain while Bill and Mom would take the car and trailer to the top and wait for us.

When we were traveling of an evening, we would first look for a railroad stock pen or fairgrounds to keep the horses. Then, if we couldn't find a motel close by, or if it was really late, we would just sleep on the ground or in our camper shell with a mattress inside. If the weather was really hot, generally we preferred sleeping outside on the ground. If it was late and too far to the next town, or we couldn't find a place to keep the horse, we would pull off the road somewhere, tie the horse to the side of the trailer, then we would sleep in the pickup shell or on the ground. Dad always made sure his horse was taken care of first, before we looked for us a place to stay. After all, his horse was what made us a living and was of the utmost importance.

During one trip through Arizona, we had a flat on the car. Bill and Mom got out the spare tire while Dad got out his dummy roping horns. He set them up on a bale of hay in front of the car and was practicing roping while Bill and Mom changed the tire. There is no telling what the people in the cars that passed us thought was happening! The image of a cowboy roping horns on a bale of hay while a woman and boy were changing a flat in the middle of the desert was quite an unusual sight, I am sure. I remember the cars slowing way down when they went past, people staring out their windows. Mom was always the one who took care of the car though, so this was not unusual in my family. Looking back, Dad could not have had a better wife than Mom, who supported his roping and way of life and did everything she could to help him so he could pursue his dream.

Another summer, as we came from California to Buffalo, Oklahoma, we had our dog Napo, a cat, two pet goldfish, and a miniature turtle that us kids had as pets. We couldn't leave any of them all summer in California, so we brought them with us. Dad wanted to go to a couple of steer ropings in New Mexico, so it was decided that Bill, Mom, and I would catch the train in New Mexico and go to Woodward, Oklahoma, where our aunt Twila could pick us up at the train depot and take us to our grandmother's house in Buffalo. We couldn't take all our pets on the train, so, with strict instructions to Dad of how to take care and feed all of them, we boarded the train. He did pretty well, as by the time he got to Buffalo, two ropings later, he arrived with all the pets in good shape except the goldfish had died because Dad hadn't changed the water, and about a week later our turtle died from a soft shell.

In 1953, the year Dad won his last World's Championship in steer roping, he gave his belt buckle to me to wear, saying it was too big for him! I wore it with pride for so many years, and recently gave it to my son, Troy, who now wears it. I always liked to tell people that Ben Johnson Jr. had one just like it, only his was for winning the World Title in team roping that same year. Of course Dad knew Ben Jr. very well. Ben even borrowed Dad's horse Cheyenne to rope steers on one year during the Ben Johnson Sr. Memorial Steer Roping at Pawhuska, Oklahoma. And 1953 was one of the years that Casey Tibbs won the saddle bronc riding championship. It was a memorable year in the sport of rodeo, with some rodeo greats winning the world in their respective events.

I was ten years old when I went with Dad to the Ben Johnson Sr. Memorial Steer Roping at Pawhuska in 1955. The night before the roping, a torrential rain had occurred, and our car got stuck in the mud that evening at the arena. It was a stick-shift car. Dad had me get in the vehicle and try to put the gears back and forth in drive and reverse while he and some others pushed on it to try to rock it out of the mud. They finally succeeded, but in the process the reverse gear was torn out. After the roping the next day, Dad was in a hurry to get to Nebraska to the Haythorn Ranch so he could get some practice roping in before some of the upcoming rodeos. On the drive to take me back to Buffalo, we stopped at my cousin's home in Woodward, where Dad mentioned that he was in a hurry to get on to Nebraska. Bud Reger, my cousin, told him that he better get the reverse gear fixed before he went driving all over the country. Dad's reply was, "I don't need to go in reverse, nobody ever got anywhere going backwards, I'm going forwards." It made sense to him, at least! Off Dad went to Nebraska, with no reverse gear in the car. It wasn't until after the Cheyenne, Wyoming, rodeo, several weeks and miles later, that Dad had the car fixed. I guess since Dad never could back up a horse trailer very well, he just didn't think reverse was something that was necessary to have.

Dad used to go up to the Haythorn Ranch north of Ogallala to stay with Waldo and Howard in the summertime between rodeos. They had a lot of cattle to practice on and a good arena. One year Mom and I went there with Dad for a short stay and I got to go out with Dad and the other cowboys to gather and brand cattle. That was an experience I always treasured, as they branded and vaccinated cattle by roping and dragging them to the fire, the way it was done in years gone by. The Haythorn's are one of the few ranches that still operate in this way today.

Every Christmas all of us would look forward to getting a Christmas card from Slim Pickens, movie star and former rodeo clown who was a close friend of Dad's. Slim would send such amusing and original cards. One Christmas he had written a cowboy's version of "T'was the Night before Christmas." The following year, 1956, at our country school's Christmas pageant, I donned my cowboy boots, hat, and jeans, and performed a rendition of it.

We didn't have a telephone while we lived at Brawley during the school months. Us kids recalled when Dad would have to use one to call someone long-distance about a roping or rodeo entries that we would all load up in the car and drive to town so Dad could use the pay phone at the Planters Hotel in Brawley. It always struck Bill and me as so funny that Dad would hold the receiver way out from him and yell into the phone. That is the way he would converse on it. He was afraid the thing would electrocute him and he didn't want to be too close to it. By 1958, we finally convinced him to let us get a telephone in the house.

SIXTEEN

Heelfly and Cheyenne, 1956–1962

When Terrapin started going lame, Ike knew he had better hurry and find another horse for back-up. In early summer of 1956, Ike went to the JA Ranch, where he had worked in his younger years, to look through their remuda. His old friend Tom Blasingame, who was still working there, had a good-looking sorrel gelding named Heelfly that he owned. He wanted Ike to come see him. The horse was out at Tom's cow camp, where he was living while working on the ranch. Over the years, from time to time, Ike would drop by to see his old cowboy friend and stay with Tom for a few days.

> Sometimes, Ike would stay a few days and ride with Tom on the ranch to check windmills and maybe brand a maverick or two as there were lots of unbranded wild cattle on the ranch then, mostly in the river pastures and the rough cedar break country. During this particular visit, Tom let Ike ride Heelfly when they went to check some windmills. All of a sudden a two year old bull maverick jumped out of the thickets and Tom told Ike to rope him so they could brand and cut him, which Ike did. Tom thought Heelfly had a very rough trot. Ike said he hadn't noticed it at all, in fact, he said that he believed he was the smoothest and best colt he had ridden in a long time. Heelfly was a four year old then. Tom gave Heelfly to Ike that day.[1]

As Ike was loading Heelfly, he pulled out a $100 hat that he had just won and gave it to his friend. A $100 hat back then in the 1950s was a very nice hat indeed. At the time, Tom's wages were $175 a month plus room and board. According to Tommy, Tom's son, Tom Blasingame was sure proud of that hat that his old friend had given him, and, likewise, Ike was sure proud of his new horse, Heelfly.

Ike steer roping on Heelfly at Yuma, Arizona, 1956.

Heelfly was a very pretty sorrel horse. His sire was Tater and his dam was Two Step, a JA mare. His AQHA registered name was Heelfly Tater. Heelfly was also a big stout horse that weighed about 1,200 pounds. He stood 15 hands tall, or five feet, but because of his muscle structure he had the appearance of being a larger horse.

Ike immediately went to training Heelfly and using him on cattle work back at Brawley, California. Within a year after he got Heelfly, Terrapin had to be euthanized.

Everett Shaw borrowed Heelfly quite a few times to rope on him, and Heelfly carried him to winning the World Champion Steer Roping title in 1959.

In the summer of 1959, Ike sold Heelfly to Earl Corbin. Earl's son, Kelly, started steer roping at an early age, and in 1964 Kelly Corbin won the steer roping at Cheyenne on Heelfly. Kelly shared the record as the youngest steer roper to win Cheyenne with Fred Lowry, a top roper in the 1920s and '30s. Both young men were only eighteen years old. Kelly and Ike won

Ike on Heelfly, Yuma, Arizona, 1956.

recognition as the youngest and the oldest to have ever won the steer roping at Cheyenne, and both won roping off horses trained by Ike.

CHEYENNE, 1957–1962

Ike was getting older, even for a steer roper, but he had never lost his love and passion for the sport. Ike liked Heelfly so much that when he heard from his old friend Tom Blasingame that Tom's son, Tommy, owned a full brother to Heelfly named Cheyenne that he wanted to sell, Ike was immediately interested. Heelfly was a bigger horse than Cheyenne, and because Ike was having some trouble mounting Heelfly, he thought it was time he looked for a shorter horse to have in reserve as he got older. In 1957 Ike made the trip once again to the JA Ranch, where Tom was still working. Cheyenne was a brown horse, about 14.3 hands tall, or 4 feet, 11 inches, but not as stout as Heelfly. That summer Ike bought him.

Ike, 1956.

Tom Blasingame, Ike's lifelong friend from ranching days. Photo credit to Douglas Kent Hall, Estate of Douglas Kent Hall, courtesy of Dawn Hall.

About every weekend there would be a jackpot team roping somewhere close around Brawley, or over into Arizona, where Ike would go and compete. Summertime was still the same—our family would leave California and head to Buffalo, where Cleo, Bill, and I would stay while Ike made the rounds of the rodeos. Between rodeos, Ike would hang out at the Haythorn Ranch in Nebraska to keep his horse "tuned," meaning trained and working well. They always had fresh cattle there to rope as Waldo, Howard, and Waldo's son, Craig, all were steer ropers. They always welcomed Ike to join them. Mom and I would go with Ike to some of the rodeos but, by this time, Bill wanted to stay at Buffalo and play Little League Baseball.

The year 1959 our family stayed at Buffalo with my aging grandmother. I attended my freshman year of high school there, and Bill was a senior. That next summer Ike got a cowboy job out on the desert at Buckeye, Arizona, taking care of cattle for rancher Jewell Turner. I attended part of my sophomore year of high school there. While we lived there, I was chosen the RCA Rodeo Queen at the annual rodeo held at Buckeye, as well as the high school's FFA rodeo queen.

Ike, sixty-seven years old, team roping, heading on Cheyenne (*at right*), with Andy Juaregui heeling, at Yuma, Arizona, 1961.

Sammie, RCA Rodeo Queen, Buckeye, Arizona, 1959.

That winter our family moved to Pendleton, Oregon, where Ike went to work for Orval McCormmach, a local rancher and horse breeder, training his horses and helping to take care of his cattle. There were lots of jackpot team ropings and barrel races held on weekends both there and at Walla Walla, Washington, that Ike and I would enter.

By 1962 my grandmother, Cleo's mother, was requiring some assistance with her declining health. So Cleo, Ike, and I moved back to Buffalo, to live with her. By then Bill was attending a trade school at Okmulgee, Oklahoma, studying to be an electrician. I was a senior in high school.

Ike decided that at sixty-eight years old, he was getting too old to rope, so he sold Cheyenne to a steer roper from New Mexico. Later that year, the cowboy had just roped his steer at the Cheyenne Frontier Days when Cheyenne suffered a heart attack and died.

RECOLLECTIONS

I loved the rodeo life and was passionate about barrel racing. When I was twelve years old, I got a permit from the Girls Rodeo Association and entered my first barrel race at Woodward, Oklahoma, riding Heelfly. He was a lot of horse for a little girl to handle, so I didn't place against the older, more experienced professional women in the sport, but I was bound and determined to be competitive. That winter when we went back to Brawley, California, I kept practicing. I had improved a lot by the next summer, and had been winning at some local barrel races. I felt like I was ready to be competitive with the professional cowgirls. Dad always encouraged me that I might as well start at the top, meaning competing with the professional women, rather than going to amateur or smaller rodeos. Of course, Dad couldn't even attend those rodeos, as professional cowboys were not allowed to compete at any rodeo other than a certified Rodeo Cowboys Association rodeo, giving me no choice but to "start at the top." I never got to test my ability with the Girls Rodeo Association women on Heelfly, as that summer Dad sold him to Earl Corbin. It was a huge disappointment for me, but luckily I had Cheyenne to start on barrels.

The summer of 1957 when Dad went to the JA Ranch to purchase Cheyenne, I was thrilled to be able to go with him. It was an experience I will cherish forever. Tom Blasingame's camp on the JA Ranch was only accessible by a day's ride on horseback. There were no roads or even cow trails. Dad and I spent a night at the line camp of another cowboy who worked for the JA ranch. It was on the rim of the Palo Duro Canyon. The cowboy loaned us a couple of horses to ride to Tom's camp. When he gave Dad instructions on how to get there, they did not involve any trails or paths, just landmarks of gullies or ridges and other landmarks to look for. He reminded us that by watching the sun or a tall ridge of a mountain, we could keep our directions straight. When riding through tall sage brush up and down hills in the canyon, it was easy to lose all sense of direction. Dad told me when you are out in country like that, the most important thing is to know your directions. Look at the sun or moon before you leave, then try to find the tallest object you can see and keep it in sight as often as you can. That way you will have a sense of where you are in relation to the object. I have used that method a few times in my life—it works! Of course, Dad had worked on this ranch. While that was over thirty-five years prior, but he had a memory of the terrain of the pastures. We were saddled and ready to go at daybreak. The cowboy's wife had packed us a lunch to take. He told us that by noon we would come to a windmill and stock tank, then go through the one and only pasture fence that we would come to, and take a more southeast direction from that point. When we got in that pasture, we did see some cattle paths to follow. It was amazing to me that Dad could ride all day long with no land markers, in dense sagebrush, and get to his destination. He confirmed what the cowboy had said, telling me we would get to the windmill around noon, eat our lunch there, then arrive at Tom's camp at 4:00. I was shocked when I got there and walked into Tom's house to see that his battery clock read 4:00 p.m.!

Tom's daughter, Nancy, happened to be staying with her dad for a few weeks at the camp during summer school break. She was my age, so we were both thrilled to get to know one another, even just for one evening. The next day, Tom and Nancy rode with us as far as the windmill. Dad and I came on back from there. Dad had bought Cheyenne, and would come back to pick him up a few weeks later.

While we lived at Pendleton, Oregon, I was able to attend a lot of jackpot barrel races riding Cheyenne. The summer of 1961 was a most memorable one for me—that summer just Dad and I went to a lot of rodeos together with Cheyenne. Dad was roping off him and I was running barrels on him. We started at Spokane, Washington. Dad entered the team roping. The rodeo grounds were built at the bottom of a steep hill with the bank of the hill made into the grandstand. During the rodeo, one of the bucking bulls got loose from the pens and ran up the steep incline into the grandstand. The bull was bucking and crashing around in the grandstand, and people were yelling and scrambling, trying to get away from the danger coming at them. It was terrifying to watch. Then Dad went racing up the hill on Cheyenne and managed to rope the bull and drag him out of the open-air stands. I was scared to death as Dad worked his way back down the hill with the bull tied hard and fast to his saddle horn, as half the time the bull was dragging Dad and Cheyenne. The bull weighed much more than they did! Cheyenne only weighed about 950 pounds. Dad sure handled his rope well, making sure that he and the bull didn't get tangled up and keeping all three of them from tumbling head over heels down the hill. Only after they got to the bottom did some other cowboys who had watched, frozen, come to the rescue and rope the bull to help Dad drag him back to the pens. After it was all over, the announcer kept talking about how only an old cowboy like Ike, who was sixty-seven years old, could have known how to handle a situation like that. He also praised Dad for preventing a tragic accident from happening that day. The announcer knew of Dad's early background working in the mountains of Arizona roping wild cattle, and he told the rodeo crowd all about it. I wish I could remember the announcer's name. He called this the wildest event he had ever witnessed—Dad coming down the side of the hill with that bull. I must say that Dad's quick thinking and the abilities he had learned in his younger days were put to the test that day.

From Spokane we went to Prineville, Oregon, then up to Bremerton, Washington. At Bremerton I placed second in the barrel race, beating out the Canadian champion barrel racer. From Bremerton, we had three days to get to Vinita, Oklahoma, to the rodeo. I was fifteen years old and had just got my drivers' permit. We got as far as the Idaho–Oregon line when Dad said he was too sleepy to keep driving, but we needed to keep going to get there in time, as this was back before the interstates had been completed. So he told me to drive and he immediately fell asleep. I drove all through Boise, Idaho, and well into Wyoming before he woke up. When he did, Dad told me he wanted to show me some pretty country, so he instructed me to turn off and head south through the western region of Colorado. I remember the road took us over the Red Mountain Pass, an extremely narrow and dangerous mountain road. It was a two-lane road but I didn't even want to look down, as we were at the top of some very steep mountains. The terrain was straight down by the sides of the road. I do remember it took us through Ironton, which is now a ghost town. The elevation was 11,018 feet. I was so scared and wanted to pull over so bad so that Dad could drive, but there were never any places to pull a pickup and trailer over to the side of the road so that we could exchange drivers. Dad had a grand time looking at the scenery and the steep mountains. I hardly saw a thing except the narrow two-lane road in front of me, I was concentrating so hard to stay on the road and not go off the edge of the steep embankments. By the time we got over the mountain pass, I was worn out and let Dad take over the driving. That was basically how I got my first real experience of driving and pulling a horse trailer, over that kind of road. That day I drove over some of the steepest and most narrow roads in the country, so I guess I can say that I learned to drive, pulling a horse trailer, by "starting at the top." It sure made me want to pay attention and keep my mind on driving! Once again, Dad seemed to think it was better to "start at the top," so to speak, in order to learn. He might have been right, as that particular time, it was either learn or die trying! I recently looked on the internet to find that route and discovered that, just as I had thought then, those roads are some of the most narrow and dangerous in the United States today. The roads that are still in existence today in that area of the mountains are now officially closed in the winter!

We made it to Vinita in time for the rodeo. They didn't have barrel racing there but Dad entered the steer roping. We had a few days to get to the prison rodeo at McAlester, so we stayed at a friend of Dad's at Nowata who had some cattle and a roping arena so Dad could get some roping practice in before the rodeo. The McAlester rodeo is always held inside the prison walls. I won second there. Jane Mayo, the World Champion barrel racer, won first. After that, Dad and I went back home to Pendleton, Oregon, where I attended my junior year in high school. I will always treasure that summer I spent with my Dad.

My brother, Bill, recalls that when he first started learning to drive he liked to drive fairly fast, like most teenagers do. When he started going too fast while Dad was riding with him, Dad wouldn't say a word but would start singing this mournful, sad song that he had sung to us as youngsters so many times. We would always cry our eyes out when he sang it. The title was "The Wreck on the Highway," recorded by Roy Acuff in 1942. It was a story about a car wreck where people died. One of the verses went, "I heard the crash on the highway, but I didn't hear nobody pray." This was enough for Bill to get the message that he was to slow down!

I remember when Dad heard about his horse Cheyenne dying at the Cheyenne Frontier Days rodeo, he cried most of the day. Dad always had a special place in his heart for his horses, as they were such a huge part of what he loved to do.

SEVENTEEN
Retirement, 1962–1968

As Ike tried to adjust to retirement, he was left to his memories and dreams of roping and cowboy life from the past. Ike did like to play poker. In the summertime after baseball practice, some of the high school boys in Buffalo would come by the house and play poker with him. Many of those boys would, in later life, remember the fun they had learning the game and playing with Ike.

By 1964, Ike and Cleo's children were married and gone from home. Bill was an electrician and lived in Enid, Oklahoma, and I had married a horse trainer, Theron Compton, and pursued the Quarter Horse shows, training and showing for the public and had moved out of state.

In 1964, Keith Lauer, a local rancher who lived at Buffalo, had two boys, C. A. and Rob, who wanted to learn to rope. C. A. was ten years old and Rob was nine. Keith told his boys that they needed to get in touch with Ike, as he would be the best person he knew of to teach them. So they did. Ike and the boys built a roping dummy with a set of steer horns and set it up in the local town park. The Lauers lived across the street from the park, and Ike lived only a block away in the little town. They would meet there after school for the next year and a half. Ike would not let them graduate to roping off a horse until they got really good at roping the stationary horns. C. A. related that in that year-and-a-half span of Ike coaching them and roping with them, he didn't recall ever seeing Ike miss at roping the dummy. While Ike spent time with the boys, he would tell them many stories of his life, one of them being how cowboys used to make their own ropes. Both boys became fascinated by Ike's career and their passion for roping increased.

During a recent conversation with Rob Lauer about his memories of Ike, he recalled one of the first team ropings that Ike took him and C. A. to, at Clayton, New Mexico, while they were both teenagers. They arrived at Clayton late in the night, and C. A. and Rob were talking about looking for a hotel to get a room, but then Ike told C. A., who was driving, to pull over by the side of the road. Ike jumped out of the pickup, reached in the back, got his bedroll out, and threw it on the ground. He crawled into it while the boys were scratching their heads, trying to figure out what Ike was doing. Soon, they realized this was where Ike intended to bed down for the night. They got their bedrolls out and did the same. Rob remembered that in the night it got really cold, so the boys decided to move their bed up into the gooseneck of the trailer. But Ike was still sound asleep on the ground. In the morning, when they woke up, they found Ike had already been up with the sun and was practicing roping his stationary horns. Both boys would later grow up to be really good ropers. C. A. has won about every major steer roping in the country over the years.

In 1965, another group of local boys developed an interest in roping. The county fairgrounds at Buffalo, the best place for them to practice, had become dilapidated and in need of some serious repairs. So Keith Lauer, Elmer Randall, Lynn Franks, Don Harmon, Dean Cochran, Vance Thompson, Delbert Lemons, Cecil Lucky, and Leo Knox, the county commissioner, the local boys who were interested in roping, and even the FFA boys made a project out of tearing down the old wooden arena and replacing it with a new pipe arena. It was truly a town project for the local people.

When the new arena and chutes were finished, they all agreed they should do something special, like organize a yearly roping. They met and decided that they would start an Ike Rude Annual Roping in honor of their local celebrity.

Their first roping was held in 1965 and just featured calf roping for the adults and junior calf roping for the kids. A couple of years later, in 1967, a jackpot team roping was added with a $100 entry fee and a four-steer average. Ike decided he would like to rope in it, so he borrowed a horse from Keith Lauer. He made a visit to Kiowa, Oklahoma, to see Clark McEntire, Reba McEntire's father, to see if he would join him as his team roping partner. Clark informed Ike that he was too busy taking care of his ranching duties and couldn't get away, but that Pecos, his son, was getting to be a fairly good roper. "Pake," as everyone called him, was fourteen years old and had been to a few local ropings and competed and had done very well. But he had never been out of the area to compete. Ike stayed a few days at the McEntire Ranch to practice with Pake, and finally decided he was capable of being his partner at the Buffalo roping. Jackie, Pake's mother, drove him and his horse to Buffalo as Pake was too young to have a driver's license yet. Pake recalled that he was scared to death, as this would be his first time to really compete with some of the "toughs" in the roping world. When the dust had settled and all four go-rounds were added up, Ike and Pecos won first in the average. It was Pake's first big win. Ike was seventy-three years old and Pecos was fourteen years old! Their win was a record that would stand for the duration of the Ike Rude Annual Roping: the oldest and the youngest to ever win the team roping.

The Ike Rude Annual Roping at Buffalo, Oklahoma, continued for a twenty-year span. It ended in 1986. In talking with C. A. about the event, he recalled that over the years it was held, it developed into a prominent event with many of the toughest ropers from all over the United States attending. It is still talked about as being one of the best-managed ropings that was ever held.

EIGHTEEN

The Rodeo Bug Bites Again, 1968–1971

Winning the team roping at Buffalo with Pake McEntire —that was all it took for Ike to want to go back to roping again.

In 1967 my husband and I purchased a small horse-training facility at Wichita, Kansas, in order to pursue our careers in training and showing performance and halter horses. Ike and Cleo lived there with us for about a year. We had built a nice roping arena where Ike put on a two-week roping school. About twenty young men began this school but only one finished. According to the one man who finished, Ike expected them to be at the barn around 4:30 in the morning, have their horse fed, saddled, and ready to start roping at daybreak. They would only take a short lunch break, and would rope till dark. The young ropers started dropping out one by one as they grew tired of keeping up that kind of pace in order to learn to rope. They just couldn't imagine how an old man of seventy-four could keep up that pace either, but Ike did. The one man who completed the school said he learned a wealth of knowledge from Ike.

In November 1968, Ike and Cleo attended the Rodeo Historical Society's annual meeting at the National Cowboy Hall of Fame in Oklahoma City. The RHS December news bulletin, *Extra*, stated: "The best show of all occurred, however, in the lobby of the Sheraton Hotel. When Ike Rude walked in, the lobby was seething with people; Everett Bowman was holding court at one side—and when they spotted each other the booming laughter could probably be heard in outer space. Both, now in their 70's, looked wonderful. Ike is even ROPING—(the words are synonymous, aren't they?)"[1]

The following year, 1969, Ike was seventy-five years old! He decided he needed a roping horse. He stopped by the Lauers' at Buffalo and told them he was on his way to see another of his old friends, Benny Binion, out at Las Vegas. When Ike got to Vegas, Benny told him to go up to his ranch in Montana and pick himself out a horse that he would give him. When Ike came back he had two horses in his trailer, but the one he got from the Binion ranch needed to be broke. He left that one at Buffalo for C. A. and Rob to break, but Ike kept the other one for himself. He called this horse "Grulla," as that was the horse's color. It was a Hancock-bred horse, which was always a preferred pedigree for a stout steer roping horse. The horse had been used some as a cutting horse, but had the reputation of putting his head down and bucking now and then. Ike said he got him off an Indian reservation in South Dakota. Ike started training Grulla for roping, but when the weather was a little nippy, that horse still had a little buck in him, and always did. He even bucked Ike off once, but at seventy-five years old, that didn't bother Ike much. He could handle it. C. A. remembered that the horse Ike left with them to break was a real outlaw that bucked them off several times, even pretty badly hurting one guy who worked for the Lauers. They called Ike and told him they thought he should get rid of that horse, so Ike told them to sell him. Ike had Grulla ready to go on the rodeo circuit in a few months, so back to steer roping and team roping he went.

That same year, 1969, Ike planned on holding another roping school at Blair, Oklahoma, with his friend Waldo Haythorn from Nebraska furnishing the cattle. The handbill stated, "Rope Plenty!" However, this school did not have many sign up to attend, and had to be cancelled. Apparently the word had gotten out regarding Ike's roping schools!

After competing at Cheyenne, Ike went to Akron, Colorado, to enter the team roping. Professor Charles "Bud" Townsend was the announcer at that rodeo. It was there he conducted the "four hour taped interview with Ike," that he referred to in his Foreword to this book.[2]

For the next two years, Ike made the rounds of the rodeos that still held steer roping and team roping. He and Cleo purchased a pickup with a topper, where they generally slept, rather than getting a motel, and a two-horse trailer. Cleo had inherited some money from her late mother and, for the first time in their marriage, Cleo wanted to buy a home. They made the decision to purchase a small home at Mangum, Oklahoma, where Ike was born and reared. In a magazine article Ike was quoted as saying, "Man's like a coyote, you jump a coyote, and he may run a hundred miles. But you watch him—he'll make a big circle, and eventually end up right back where he started. That's me. I'm back in Mangum after a sixty-five year circle."[3] By this time, Cleo was growing tired of traveling and, since she had her new home, she didn't always join Ike in his travels during these two years. She still always encouraged him to go and do what he enjoyed. Ike did not win much during this time, but he was still competitive and had a lot of fun.

Ike, age seventy-five, putting a saddle on Grulla at Pendleton Round-Up, 1969. The picture came out in the *East Orgonian* newspaper

In 1970 the Matador Ranch's Alamositas Division at Channing, Texas, held a reunion that included an invitational senior calf roping and team roping. It was open to any cowboy fifty-five years old and older who had ever worked on the ranch. Ike decided to go compete against them to see if he could give the younger cowboys, some of them twenty-two years younger than him, a run for their money. He did just that and came out the winner in the calf roping and second in the team roping. Ike was presented with a tooled and stamped trophy saddle and breast collar for winning the all-around title. He also received a pair of Adolph Bayers-made spurs for being the oldest active cowboy present who had worked for the Matadors. How ironic that he was given awards for his roping now after getting in trouble for roping too much on this same ranch fifty-six years prior!

Ike's last rodeo was the Cheyenne Frontier Days in 1971. Ike was featured on the front page of the *Sunday Empire*, the magazine of the *Denver Post*, with an article titled "Is 77 Too Old For a Rodeo Cowboy, Not If Your Name Is Ike Rude."[4] The Denver newspaper always liked to interview and

Ike, eighty-one years old in 1975, shown with the Matador saddle and spurs he won when he was seventy-seven, roping at the Matador Ranch Cowboy Reunion.

write stories on Ike when he competed at Cheyenne. That year they featured his life story in their article.

It was reported that year that Ike made the short go at Cheyenne, roping steers. Going into the finals he had the steer roped, tripped, and was back tying him, when all of a sudden his horse, Grulla, went to pitching and ran off with the steer, knocking Ike out of the average. For just a few seconds, it looked like the seventy-seven-year-old cowboy was going to beat his own record at Cheyenne, Wyoming, to be the oldest to ever win the steer roping! This would be Ike's final rodeo to compete. It was a fitting ending, for, as a young boy, Cheyenne had always been Ike's favorite rodeo.

After having been on the road for the past three years, Ike was starting to feel his aches and pains, and arthritis was taking its toll on his body. Once again, he decided to sell his horse and trailer, and retire again. This time he had a permanent home to go to at Mangum, Oklahoma.

NINETEEN

Recognition throughout the United States, 1965–2018

ke's rodeo career had lasted for sixty-one years—from 1910 to 1971—and had carried him throughout the United States, Canada, Mexico, and England. In so doing, he had set many records, as well as helping to establish and develop the sport as we know it today. Although rodeo has made many changes throughout the years, Ike participated in its earliest days and he continued as it was changing until 1971. In his career he roped in all three roping events: calf, steer, and team roping. Ike has been recognized with many honors over the years in various states.

The Ike Rude Annual Roping at Buffalo, Oklahoma, was held from 1965 to 1986.

In 1965, the National Cowboy Hall of Fame (now the National Cowboy and Western Heritage Museum) was opened in Oklahoma City. The hall's board members voted each year on who would be inducted into the National Rodeo Hall of Fame. This procedure did not set well with the Rodeo Cowboys Association (RCA), as they had no voice in the selection of their own peers. The National Cowboy Hall of Fame was never limited to professional rodeo as defined by the CTA, RCA, or PRCA—many other western culture items and prominent people were added, from art and artifacts to movie stars, singers, ranchers, and people who have promoted the western life. The section for the rodeo cowboys would become the National Rodeo Hall of Fame. Yet even before the Hall of Fame had been completed and opened, many of the rodeo cowboys kept saying that Ike Rude should be the first to be inducted into it. They kept arguing with the museum's director, Dean Krakel, and board members that it should be the cowboys who had the right to vote on their own peers regarding who should be honored in the rodeo division, not the board of directors of the museum and hall, who were largely bankers and wealthy ranchers. They also did

Inside they put an "eagles heart"
And the courage of a lion,
Then he set out on a long career
A ropin' and a tyin'.

I don't know that he started out
To make himself a name,
Or if he meant to rope his way
Into the "Hall of Fame".

If so, they had to change the rules
To get him in, here's why,
The powers that be all had in mind
That he would never die.

There might be a "cowboy heaven"
He could get into, of course,
But he won't make a deal up there
Unless they'll take his horse.

No need for him to go "below"
Hell, man, he wouldn't dare,
He'd rope and tie the devil
Then they'd run him out of there.

Well, maybe there's another place
But that's another story,
Meanwhile he'll just stay on earth
And bask in all his glory.

The following year, 1975, the little town of Mangum, Oklahoma, honored Ike by recognizing his accomplishments at the Old Greer County Museum of noted people and pioneers who were from that area. They erected a granite monument for Ike on the museum's grounds. Ike's father, Sam Rude, has a granite monument there as well. The town also decided to rename the street on which Ike and Cleo lived to "Ike Rude Avenue." To this day there is a room in the museum dedicated to Ike with many photographs, articles, and some of his archives and artifacts.

On January 31, 1975, the Mangum Chamber of Commerce held a banquet to honor Ike. Two hundred fifty people attended the little country town celebration. Victor Wickersham, Oklahoma state representative, was there to announce that at the next Oklahoma state legislature meeting, they would be honoring and recognizing Ike. The Oklahoma House of Representatives issued a citation congratulating Ike for his rodeo skills

Ike and Cleo stand beside Ike's granite monument at the Old Greer County Museum and Hall of Fame in Mangum, Oklahoma, 1979.

and for becoming the first living cowboy to be inducted into the National Rodeo Hall of Fame. On February 5, 1975, a resolution, adopted by the Oklahoma Senate and the House of Representatives, was issued that read: "That the many outstanding accomplishments of Ike Rude, and the resulting honor he has brought to Oklahoma, be and hereby are commended to the annals of the great state of Oklahoma, and offered as inspiring examples to all who seek excellence." This resolution was issued to be a permanent record in not only the Oklahoma legislature, but the National Archives in Washington, DC; the National Cowboy Hall of Fame; the Oklahoma Historical Museum; each city and school library in Greer, Harmon, and Beckham Counties; the Old Greer Museum in Mangum; the museum in Hollis, Oklahoma; the Old Town Museum in Elk City, Oklahoma; and the Granite Museum in Granite, Oklahoma.

On October 13, 1977, Ike was the guest of honor at the O. S. Ranch Roping and Art Exhibit that was held at Post, Texas, and was given a plaque to reflect this honor.

By 1978 the town of Mangum decided to organize a celebration and call it "Ike Rude Day." A jackpot calf roping and barrel racing was sponsored, as well as an all-out town celebration that would last three days and included an art show and flea market, with vendors coming and setting up tents all around the town square. Activities included all sorts of races and entertainment for the children, dancing, and rattlesnake hunts. This became an annual event for several years.

The Pendleton Round-up at Pendleton, Oregon, honored Ike by making him grand marshal of the 1978 festivities.

In May 1979 Ike was honored, with other rodeo cowboys, in the Oklahoma State Senate as one of the "rodeo greats" from Oklahoma who had contributed greatly to recognition in the rodeo arena.

Also in 1979 Ike was inducted into the ProRodeo Hall of Fame in Colorado Springs, Colorado, along with his horses Baldy and Bullet.

In the year 1981 Ike was inducted in the Pendleton Round-up Hall of Fame, in Pendleton, Oregon.

Clem McSpadden, renowned rodeo announcer and Oklahoma state senator, asked Ike in 1981 to attend his annual ranch roping held at Bushyhead, Oklahoma, and to be a guest of honor along with other living legends, including rodeo greats Barton Carter, Buck Goodspeed, Forman Faulkner, Monroe Veach, Joe Crow, and a youngster named Freckles Brown.

Also in 1981, the Woodward Elks Rodeo at Woodward, Oklahoma, honored Ike by asking him to be the parade marshal and guest of honor during their rodeo.

The museum in the town of Buffalo, Oklahoma, was where Ike had his saddle he won at Cheyenne on display for several years. That saddle has now been restored, and is displayed back at the National Cowboy and Western Heritage Museum in the American Rodeo Gallery in Oklahoma City, where it was first displayed many years ago.

POSTHUMOUS HONORS

In 2004, Ike was inducted into the Cheyenne Frontier Days Hall of Fame and Old West Museum at Cheyenne, Wyoming.

In 2005, Ike was inducted into the Will Rogers Stampede Rodeo Hall of Fame in Claremore, Oklahoma.

In 2018, Ike was honored into the Ben Johnson Cowboy Museum in Pawhuska, Oklahoma.

TWENTY

One Final Attempt, 1983

y 1983 Ike hadn't been on a horse in twelve years. His body was old and riddled with arthritis and his hands and fingers were beginning to be bent out of shape, but his spirit and mind were very much intact. The desire to rope had not faded. At eighty-nine years old he made up his mind, once again, to get off that bed and go back to roping!

Ike didn't have a horse, trailer, pickup, or saddle. Rather, he had a saddle, but it was sitting at the National Cowboy Hall of Fame in Oklahoma City! Ike figured he could borrow some cowboy's horse to rope on. Heaven knows that enough cowboys had always borrowed his horses throughout his lifetime. Getting on a horse shouldn't be a problem—just as when he came out of retirement the first time, he'd use a stool to mount his horse before riding into the arena to rope. He generally would lead his horse out of the arena after dismounting to tie his steer. Getting off to tie the steer was no problem in Ike's mind, for, as he said, "Anyone can fall off!" And he had kept a lot of his ropes.

Ike and Cleo headed to Oklahoma City to the National Cowboy Hall of Fame to get his saddle. When they arrived, Willard Porter, the rodeo author who was Ike's friend who had written a slew of articles on Ike and other cowboys, was working there at that time. He tried to talk Ike out of it, but Ike would have none of it. He was going back to roping! Luckily, Ike had had the forethought, years prior, to only loan his saddle to the hall, not give it to them. Willard followed Ike out to the car as they loaded his saddle. Willard made Ike sign a release stating that if Ike got hurt, he would bring the saddle back to the hall so they could keep it on display. Ike signed the agreement after giving Willard the assurance that the saddle would not be coming back, as he never had been hurt in his life from roping and didn't intend to be now!

It was wintertime when this occurred and the steer ropings hadn't started yet for the summer season. Ike never was able to rope again, after getting his saddle back from the National Cowboy Hall of Fame. His body was just too feeble and not able to cooperate with his mind.

RECOLLECTIONS

In March 1983 I was working for Baker Oil Tools as region secretary in Oklahoma City. One afternoon my work phone rang and it was Mom saying, "You will never guess what your Dad wants to do." I had no idea since he had basically been lying on a bed the past ten years and was becoming feeble. "He wants to go back to roping," she said. I told her this was impossible and if he attempted it, he was going to get hurt. She said she knew that, but if Ike wanted to do it, there was no stopping him. Once again, my Mom was going to support Dad in anything he wanted to do! Unbelievable! I went through all the scenarios of how it couldn't be done at his age, and I was frantic to think of what could happen if he attempted it. But Dad still went and got his saddle.

Over the next couple of months, I kept in contact on a regular basis, to see if Dad had attempted to go to a rodeo yet. Luckily he hadn't, but I was in constant anticipation of what would occur next.

Ike at age eighty-nine in 1983, reminiscing of days gone by. A portrait of him roping hangs on the wall above.

TWENTY ONE

The Last Round-Up, 1983–1985

RECOLLECTIONS

Once again, in June 1983, I get another phone call from Mom with the same amazing question of "Guess what your Dad wants to do?" Mom informed me that Dad wanted to accept Christ as his Lord and Savior and be baptized in the First Christian Church in Mangum. I could have fallen out of my chair from surprise. We kids and Mom had attended church many times on Sundays when we weren't at a rodeo, and my brother and I had attended a little country Methodist church quite regularly when we lived at Brawley, California. Mom had tried all her life to get Dad to attend with us, but Dad always said the roof would cave in if he ever went to church. Yet as a boy growing up, Dad's mother had seen to it that he went to church with her and his sisters. Apparently Dad must have paid some attention, as he sure remembered lots of old-time hymns that he would sing as we traveled. Dad said he wanted Bill and I there when he was baptized.

On June 26, 1983, Dad made his public confession of accepting Jesus Christ as his Lord and Savior. The First Christian Church believes in baptizing with total immersion. Dad had to be helped into the water. After coming up out of the water, he shook like a dog with the biggest grin on his face. The first thing he said was, "Boy, I feel so much better; I should have done this years ago!" He was grinning and so happy the rest of the day. It was like the weight of the world had been lifted off his shoulders, and indeed it had.

Even though Dad had never attended church with us prior, I often wondered how much in the past Dad might have thought about the Lord. One time comes to mind out at Post, Texas, in 1977 when Dad was invited to be guest of honor during the O. S. Ranch Roping and Art Exhibit. I had gone out to be with my folks. On Sunday morning they had a "cowboy church" service that was held outside. Mom convinced Dad to come with us. After the first prayer, Dad got up and went back to the car. Mom and I stayed for the rest of the service. Afterward, Mom asked him why he left, as she thought it was a good service. Dad's reply was, "I don't think much of it if the preacher and a majority of the cowboys did not remove their hats during the service." Dad had done so, and he felt, out of respect to the Lord, even if you were outside, that should be done. I know that in current times this is not done sometimes at cowboy churches anymore, but I feel Dad was right in his thinking.

For the next few days Mom said Dad was happier than she had seen him in a long time. He just kept talking about how much better he felt and how he should have been baptized years before.

Then, a little over one month later, I got a call from Mom in the middle of the night. She said Dad had been taken by ambulance to the hospital in Mangum. He was hemorrhaging internally and they couldn't get it stopped. She said I should come quickly. It took me about three hours to drive from my home at Guthrie, Oklahoma, to Mangum, but I arrived at the hospital early that morning. When I arrived, Dad was still bleeding uncontrollably. They had given him the maximum amount of blood transfusions that a body can endure in a given time, but blood was leaving his body quicker than they could put it in. The doctor arrived shortly to inform us of the prognosis. If they did nothing, Dad would bleed to death probably in an hour or two. The only solution was to go in and do exploratory surgery to see if they could find the source of the bleeding and stop it. But, because Dad was eighty-nine years old, and already his body was in an extremely weakened condition from losing so much blood, the doctor did not give him much of a chance of survival. Dad insisted on knowing what the odds were. The doctor told him if they did nothing, it was a 100 percent chance he would die. If they did surgery, it was about a 95 to 5 percent, with the 5 percent being the chances of survival. Since Dad had been a gambler most of his life, he immediately made the decision to go for it. For him it was a no-brainer of which way to go. After talking with Dad, the doctor called Mom and me outside the room. He told us to go back in and say our good-byes, as it would be a miracle if Dad could pull through the surgery because of his compromised condition. We didn't tell Dad what the doctor told us, but went back in the room. Dad was in the best of spirits when we walked back in. He was clear-headed, and we visited with him while the doctor was getting things ready for the surgery. All of a sudden we noticed Dad wasn't paying attention to what we were talking about. He was squinting his eyes and looking up at the ceiling, like he was watching something. Mom said, "Ike, what are you looking at?" Dad said he was watching a bunch of cowboys moving cattle in a lush green grass meadow. They were riding some of the best-looking horses he had ever seen in his life. Mom immediately knew that he was having a vision. Dad was explaining everything so thoroughly, but kept asking Mom and me if we couldn't see it also. We kept telling him that no, we couldn't see it. It was so very clear to him. He just couldn't understand why we weren't seeing it also. Mom asked him if any of the horses were his old horses—could one of them be Baldy, maybe? About that time Dad lifted himself up in bed to a sitting position. I really don't know where he got the strength to do this in his extremely weakened condition. By doing this, he was trying to get closer so he could see more clearly. He then started laughing and told us he was seeing all sorts of wild animals romping and playing with one another: a bear cub and a mountain lion, deer, elk, bobcats, dogs, all sorts of animals were running around playing and having a good time. What really threw Mom and me was that he even described a camel joining in on all the fun! He eventually laid back down and said that no, he was not able to get close enough to identify the horses or the cowboys riding them, and the vision was fading. About that time the nurse came in to take Dad to surgery. Dad was completely relaxed and happy.

Mom and I waited in the hospital chapel for the next couple of hours. Finally, the doctor came in and informed us that he had just witnessed a miracle. He could not believe it—though he had found and repaired the rupture that was causing the bleeding, he honestly had never expected Ike to regain consciousness—but he had, and he seemed to be talking rationally. We could go in and see him now.

Dad was bedridden after this and Mom could not bring him home to care for him, so he went to live at the veterans' home at Clinton, Oklahoma, in August 1983. Mom would make the one-hundred-forty-mile round trip from Mangum to visit him almost daily. His mind was still good and his memory was still so clear! He could still tell you about every rodeo he had ever been to and generally what his time was to tie this steer or that calf. For more than a year she would test him to see if he remembered the vision he had prior to surgery. He would always recite it, almost word for word, the

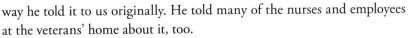

way he told it to us originally. He told many of the nurses and employees at the veterans' home about it, too.

One of the poems that Dad always loved and recited many times as we "were going down the road" connects so appropriately with his vision:

The Cowboy's Horse
Unknown

It's hard to believe you are really gone
Across the divide to the range beyond
But your once-proud head is quiet now,
You've held your last herd an' beat your last cow.

I bow my head as the fact goes home,
That of all the cowponies I may ever own,
I'll never find one more faithful than you
Or more willing to do, what I want him to do.

I'll always recall, with a lump in my throat,
What a job you could do on the end of a rope.
An' how quiet you'd work cutting cows in a herd
Yet how fast you could be when I gave you the word.

You were more than a horse, you were a friend
Who always stood by me right to the end.
But I guess the Big Boss on the range in the blue
Was badly in need of a horse like you.

So he borrowed you "Pard" for a roundup or two
On that swell range of his, up there in the blue.
Angel cowpunchers will ride you up there
But I know they will give you the finest of care.

Until my work is done on the range down here
And I've turned my last cow and roped my last steer
When I cross that last river, I know you will be
All saddled and waitin,' on the bank just for me.

In talking with C. A. Lauer recently, he told me that he, Rob, and their father, Keith, went to visit Dad at the veterans' home. As they were leaving, Dad called Rob and C. A. back into the room and told them, "Don't be afraid to ride into the wind."

By the last part of 1984, Dad's body was growing very weak and his mind had finally started slipping. He had a crippling case of arthritis and was starting to fade away from us. On January 25, 1985, I got the call to come to the veterans' home at Clinton, that it wouldn't be long before Dad passed. When I got there Dad was already in a coma and unresponsive. I was amazed at how strong his heart was beating, though. It was so strong it was moving the bed with every beat. After watching him for an hour or so, I went outside to pray and think what I should do, if anything. I had the need to go back into the room and tell him this: I leaned over where he could hear me and, before Mom came back in the room, I said, "It's okay Daddy, go to Jesus . . . I will see that Mom is taken care of." About forty-five minutes later Dad quietly passed away.

Since then, I have been told by nurses who have witnessed death that they have seen this happen before. They believe sometimes the person is fighting so hard to stay alive because of ties to their loved ones here on earth, that letting them know it is okay to leave them, that loved ones left behind will be taken care of, helps a person make the transition to the other side. Also, as we know, people who have been in comas and come out of them could sometimes hear and remember what was said to them.

We had Dad's funeral on a very blustery, icy, snowy day on January 27, 1985, at Mangum. There weren't many old-time rodeo cowboys there apart from Willard Porter, who said he figured that Ike, at age ninety, almost ninety-one, had outlived them all. Clark and Jackie McEntire were there, but Clark was much younger than Ike. Ike had been the best of friends with and was close to the same age as Clark's dad, John, but John had died years before. Jim Snively and family attempted to come but the ice storm was so severe they had to turn around and go back to Pawhuska.

At Dad's funeral, Mom gave each of the casket bearers a copy of "The Cowboy's Horse" in remembrance of Ike Rude.

Willard Porter had written a fitting article about Ike years prior:

> In his prime, Ike stood five feet, five inches tall and never weighed much more than 160 pounds soaking wet with muddy water from the Red River. Somebody once said that he had more real cowboy know-how inside that small frame than you could find in 100 drugstores on 100 Saturday nights. And he got that way, he will allow, by roping everything that moved into his line of vision. . . . [Mr. Porter asked:] "Ike, it always seemed to me that you were one of the happiest guys in the rodeo game. I mean you always seemed to be enjoying what

you were doing . . . you were always enjoying that roping more than anyone I can recall. And I can recall a few good ones like Toots Mansfield, Everett Shaw, Jess Goodspeed, Buckshot Sorrells, Troy Fort, John D. Dalton, and a few others like Shoat Webster, Cotton Lee, and Jack Skipworth. Tell me, how do you account for that? Why did you enjoy roping so much?" Ike's reply was "I always liked it since I was a little kid and liked it better and better the older I got."[1]

Clem McSpadden came and gave the eulogy: "Ike was the last of his breed; a true old-time cowboy that had crossed from the era of working on some of the largest ranch outfits in the West in the days of the Chuck Wagon, into competing as a rodeo cowboy and had set records all along the way in doing so."

Ike loved to rope with a passion, and I think it is fair to say that he probably roped more cattle in his lifetime, and had more fun doing it, than any person that ever lived, or possibly ever will.

ACKNOWLEDGMENTS

I am forever grateful for the encouragement and support that I received from many friends I relied on for advice, critique, general support, and encouragement, as I struggled to write this book.

I want to give a special thank you to my brother, Bill Rude, whom I spent hours calling and questioning about both my and his recollection of events that happened during our childhood years. We reminisced through many memories and discussions of what Dad had told us pertaining to his life before we wore born in order for me to try to get the real story. I give thanks for his encouragement, help, and support.

Willard Porter's articles and chapters in books about Ike were incredibly beneficial and helped tremendously with this endeavor, as well as George Williams's articles, and others, for which I give credit throughout the book.

A very special thank you goes to Professor Charles R. Townsend, known in rodeo as "Bud," for spending hours talking with me about the book and advising me. Also, a big thank you to him for doing a four-hour taped interview with Ike in 1969. Had it not been for this taped interview, I would not have been able to compile much of the information that forms my first few chapters of Ike's ranching days. Also I am grateful to Texas Tech University at Lubbock, Texas, for making available to me the tape recordings, which are part of their Oral Southwest Collection of Texas History. These are kept in their audio library and are available to the public.

I am so appreciative to Gail Woerner, the Rodeo Historical Society's historian and publisher of many rodeo articles and books pertaining to rodeo. Also a big thank you goes out to Chuck Schroeder, who has been involved in various aspects of Western culture throughout his career. These two people reviewed and critiqued my manuscript and were instrumental in recommending that it be published with Texas A&M University Press. Their critique and advice were invaluable to me.

Last, but certainly not least, a huge thank you to Michael R. Grauer, McCasland Chair of Cowboy Culture and Curator of Cowboy Collections and Western Art at the National Cowboy and Western Heritage Museum in Oklahoma City, Oklahoma. It was a gift that fell from Heaven when I met him, and he showed interest and offered to help me to get my book published. He has provided so much help and support, and has been both editor and contributing writer in regard to an expanded history of the ranches where Ike worked and also World War I, in which he served. He has taken hours out of his very busy schedule to work with me. Without him and his contributions, this book would not be what it is, nor would it have been available to be distributed in the places that he opened doors for it to be. His valuable expertise and contacts have taken it in a direction I could not have imagined. I am so thankful for his interest in this project.

I will be forever grateful to Texas A&M University Press and to the Paup Ranching Heritage Foundation for being the publisher of my book on the life story of Ike Rude.

APPENDIX 1
Prominent People

- NRHF indicates National Rodeo Hall of Fame at The National Cowboy & Western Heritage Museum, (NCWHM), Oklahoma City, Oklahoma. Where noted below, information is credited to the Museum.

- PRHF indicates ProRodeo Hall of Fame and Museum of the American Cowboy, Colorado Springs, Colorado.

- There are numerous other hall of fames that this list does not contain, in which the following cowboys and others are enshrined.

Carl Arnold (1898–1973)—A prominent steer roper in the 1930s and 1940s. He won Pendleton in 1930 and won Cheyenne in 1930, 1940, and 1947. He was also very competitive in calf and team roping. 1985 inducted in NRHF.

Bob Askin (1900–1973)—He won many of the major rodeos in the 1920s and 1930s, competing in Saddle Bronc Riding. 1977 inducted in NRHF.

Tex Austin (1887–1941)—Early day pioneer as a rodeo producer throughout the United States as well as taking his rodeo to London, England in the year 1924 and again in 1934. He also produced the first rodeo to be held in Madison Square Garden, New York City, New York. 1976 inducted in NRHF.

Gene Autry (1907–1998)—A western singer, songwriter, actor, musician and rodeo producer. Also owner of a Major League Baseball team. He has been enshrined in several halls of fames for acting, singing and also was 1972 inducted in Hall of Great Western Performers and in 1980 Hall of Great Westerners at NCWHM. 1979 inducted in PRHF.

Hugh Bennett (1905–1994)—World Champion Steer Wrestler 1932, World

Champion Steer Roper 1938. Hugh was the leader of organizing the "Cowboys Turtle Assoc." Also was one of the founders of the American Quarter Horse Assn. and served as a past president. 1977 inducted in NRHF. 1979 inducted in PRHF.

Benny Binion (1901–1989)—He raised a lot of top bucking horses. Benny was a huge promotor and sponsor of rodeo and rodeo contestants throughout the years. He was the person that got the Natonal Finals Rodeo moved to Las Vegas. Is most well-known for his Binion Casino in Las Vegas. 1988 inducted in the PRHF.

Tom Blasingame (1898–1989)—A multi-honored ranching cowboy that spanned for 73 years. Worked most of this time for the JA Ranch in the Texas Panhandle.

Everett Bowman (1899–1971)—All-Around Champion Cowboy 1935, 1937; Steer Wrestling World Champion 1930, 1933, 1935, 1938; Calf-Roping World Champion 1929, 1935, 1937; Steer Roping World Champion 1937. Instrumental in the organization of the "Cowboy's Turtle Assn." 1955 inducted in NRHF. 1979 inducted in PRHF.

John Bowman (1899–1959)—1936 All-Around Champion Cowboy, Steer Roping World Champion 1933, 1936. He was also a major contender in calf roping and steer wrestling. 1955 inducted in NRHF.

Louis Brooks (1916–1983)—All-Around Champion Cowboy 1943, 1944. Saddle Bronc World Champion 1943, 1944; Bareback Bronc World Champion 1942, 1944. 1955 Inducted in NRHF. 1991 inducted in PRHF.

Clyde Burk (1913–1945)—World Champion Calf Roper 1936, 1938, 1942, and 1944. 1966 inducted in NRHF.

Jiggs Burk (1920–1978)—A calf roper in the 1940s and 1950s. Jiggs was a brother to Clyde Burk.

Tom Burnett (1871–1938)—Owner and manager of the famed Four Sixes

Ranch (6666) in Texas. 1978 Inducted into Hall of Great Westerners at NCWHM.

J. Ellison Carroll (1862–1942)—Proclaimed Steer Roping Champion from 1904–1913. 1976 inducted into NRHF.

Barton Carter (1894–1991) —A member of the Cowboys Turtle Assoc. as well as RCA. Steer-roper, and calf roper throughout the 1920s and 1930s. Also a noted Quarter Horse trainer.—2005 Inducted into NRHF.

Foghorn Clancy (1882–1958)—A rodeo announcer and historian for six decades. He was known for his loud, booming voice. He announced all the major rodeos during his career. 1991 inducted into NRHF.

Breezy Cox (1900–1960)—A top All-Around hand competing in saddle bronc riding and calf roping from 1920–1940. Also made a living as a working cowboy in Arizona and New Mexico. 1982 inducted into NRHF.

Bing Crosby (1903–1977)—A most popular American actor and singer from 1930 to 1954. He recorded over 1600 songs and starred in over 70 feature motion picture films. An Academy Award winner, Grammy Global Achievement Award, and one of only thirty-three people to have three stars on the Hollywood Walk of Fame, are just some of Bing's accomplishments.

Bob Crosby (1897–1947)—He won the All-Around title at Cheyenne and Pendleton in 1925, 1927, and 1928 by competing in steer roping, bronc riding, steer wrestling, and wild horse racing. His main event was steer roping and won many matched ropings against the best of his time. 1966 inducted in NRHF. 1983 inducted PRHF. No relation to the famous band leader and movie actor.

Andy Curtis (1912–1979)—A competitive Saddle Bronc rider and Steer Wrestler. He won the steer wrestling at Chicago in 1938, 1939, and 1940. 1986 inducted in NRHF.

Dizzy Dean (1910–1974)—Major League Baseball player as Pitcher for St.

Louis Cardinals, Chicago Cubs, and St. Louis Browns during the 1930s

Chock Dyer—He roped calves and steers from 1919 to 1948. He won the steer roping at Dewey, Oklahoma in 1943. Chock was from Bartlesville, OK.

Troy Fort (1917–1993)—World Champion Calf Roper 1947, 1949. He also was a steer roper to be reckoned with. He was the last owner of the famous horse "Baldy". 1986 inducted in NRHF. 1979 inducted in PRHF.

Lou Gehrig (1903–1941)—Major League Baseball Player for New York Yankees as First Baseman from 1923–1939.

Charles Goodnight (1836–1929)—An American rancher, known mainly for founding first cattle ranch in the Texas Panhandle. 1955 inducted into The Hall of Great Westerners at the NCWHM.

Jess Goodspeed (1912–1983)—A prominent calf roper from the mid 1930s through the 1950s. 1987 inducted in NRHF.

Bill Hedge (1916–2002)—Bill broke horses, in his early years, for Ronald Mason. Later, he created Blue Ribbon Downs, the first pari-mutual horserace track in Oklahoma. He also was a very successful racehorse trainer.

C. B. Irwin (1875–1934)—Producer of a Wild West show, then later was a livestock contractor and rodeo producer. He furnished livestock for, and helped to organize, the early years of Cheyenne Frontier Days. He won the steer roping at Cheyenne in 1906. He was the owner of the famous bucking horse, "Steamboat." 1975 inducted into NRHF. 1979 inducted in PRHF.

Andy Jauregui (1903–1990)—Rodeo Stock Contractor. Was also World Champion Steer Roper in 1931 and World Champion Team Roper in 1934. Andy also worked in the motion picture industry as a stuntman and double. 1979 inducted in NRHF. 1979 inducted in PRHF.

Ben Johnson Jr. (1918–1996)—World Champion Team Roper 1953. He was a motion picture star and won an Oscar in the film, "The Last Picture Show". He appeared in several movies throughout his career. 1961 inducted in NRHF, 1982 inducted in Hall of Great Performers at NCWHM, and 1979 inducted in PRHF.

Ben Johnson Sr. (1896–1952)—Prominent steer roper in the 1920s. He won Cheyenne in 1922, 1923, and 1926. He won the steer roping at Pendleton in 1927. Foreman for Bernard-Chapman Ranch in Osage County, Oklahoma. He was the father of Ben "Son" Johnson Jr. who became a famous movie actor and also a World Champion Team Roper. 1961 inducted into Hall of Great Westerners at the NCWHM.

Colonel W.T. Johnson (1875–1943)—Producer of many major rodeos throughout the United States in the mid 1930s. 2011 inducted in NRHF.

Cotton Lee—A steer roper in the 1940s from Clovis, New Mexico. He won the World Championship in Steer Roping in 1946 in the International Rodeo Assoc.

Robert E. Lee (1807–1870)—An American Confederate General, best known as a commander of the Confederate States Army during the American Civil War.

Fred Lowry (1892–1956)—A top steer roper from 1909–1948. During this time he won the steer roping at Cheyenne six times and calf roping once. 1987 inducted into NRHF.

Toots Mansfield (1914–1998)—Toots was the man to beat in calf roping throughout the 1940s. He was World Champion Calf Roper in 1939, 1940, 1941, 1943, 1945, 1948 and 1950. 1981 inducted in NRHF.

Pepper Martin (1904–1965)—Played Major League Baseball for St. Louis Cardinals as Third Baseman and Outfielder during 1930s and early 1940s

Ronald Mason (1890–1985)—A prominent horseman and breeder of great roping horses in the 1930s and 1940s. Many cowboys bought their roping horses from Mr. Mason, which included Ike Rude who purchased both "Baldy" and "Buster" from him. His stallions included the horses "Beggar Boy" and "Oklahoma Star", who was inducted in 1992 in the American Quarter Horse Assn. Hall of Fame.

Clark McEntire (1927–2014)—World Champion Steer Roper 1957, 1958 and 1961. Father of Reba McEntire, country music singer. 1988 inducted in NRHF. 1979 inducted in PRHF, 2019 inducted in Hall of Great Westerners in NCWHM.

Clay McGonagill (1879–1921)—Over his lifetime he won over 500 contests in steer roping. He roped in the early 1900s. 1975 inducted into NRHF.

Clem McSpadden (1925–2008)—A most premier rodeo announcer for many years. Announced many of the major rodeos throughout the United States and also Calgary, Canada. He was National Finals Rodeo Announcer for 20 years. He served as President of the Rodeo Cowboys Association. In addition to his rodeo career, Clem also served as an Oklahoma State Senator for 18 years and in the U.S. House of Representatives until his death. 1989 inducted in NRHF. 1990 inducted in PRHF, and "Legends of Pro Rodeo" at the PRCA Hall of Fame in 2008.

King Merritt (1894–1953)—A consistently top competitor in steer wrestling, calf and steer roping for three decades. Won steer roping at Pendleton in 1925 and 1935 and World Champion in 1942. Was a founding member of the AQHA. 1977 inducted into NRHF.

Irby Mundy (1889–1973)—Worlds Champion Calf Roper in 1934. Irby also was a steer roper and steer wrestler during this time. For most of his years he lived in Colorado Springs, Colorado.

Homer Pettigrew (1915–1997)—World Champion Steer Wrestler for 6 years in the 1940s. He dominated that event for a decade. He also competed in calf roping and won many major rodeos in that also. In 1949 he was Reserve World Champion in Calf Roping. 1979 inducted in PRHF.

Slim Pickens (1919–1983)—Steer Wrestler, and both Bareback and Saddle

Bronc Riding were Slims events. He was also a prominent Rodeo Clown and Bullfighter. He is best known for his acting career in motion pictures starting in 1950 and starred in many productions for several years. 1986 inducted in NRHF, 1982 inducted in National Hall of Great Westerners at NCWHM. 2005 inducted in PRHF.

Willard Porter (1920–1992)—Prominent rodeo journalist and book writer on rodeo and rodeo cowboys. Former Director of the National Cowboy Hall of Fame between 1979–1986, Editor of The Quarter Horse Journal from 1949–1953. Publisher of "Hoofs and Horns" mid 1950s. Historian on rodeo cowboys. 1991 inducted in NRHF.

Will Rogers (1879–1935)—World famous stage and film actor, vaudeville performer, cowboy, humorist, newspaper columnist, and social commentator from Oklahoma in the 1920s and 1930s. Will made 71 films, (50 silent and 21 talk). He had a vaudeville rope act that he performed in the Ziegfeld Follies. He was killed in a plane crash with Wiley Post. Since then he has been honored throughout the World for his accomplishments which are too numerous to list. In 1955 he was inducted in the Hall for Great Westerners at the NCWHM.

Babe Ruth (1895–1948)—Famous Major League Baseball player from 1914–1935.

Everett Shaw (1908–1979)—World Champion Steer Roper in 1945, 1946, 1948, 1951, 1959, and 1962. He won the calf roping at Madison Square Garden in 1934, 1936, 1939. He was an original member of the Cowboys Turtle Assn. 1980 inducted into NRHF. 1979 inducted in PRHF.

Jim Snively (1911–1998)—Calf Roper from 1929 through the 1950s, winning at one time or another about every major rodeo. In 1956 he was World Champion Steer Roper and runner up in 1952 and 1958. Jim won the first National Finals Rodeo in steer roping. 2020 inducted in NCHF.

Buckshot Sorrells (1913–1977)—Competed in Steer Roping, Steer Wrestling, Calf Roping and Team Roping, winning the World Championship title in Team Roping in 1950. He competed from the 1930s until the early 1950s. 1990 inducted in NRHF.

Casey Tibbs (1929–1990)—Considered by many to be the best bronc rider of all time. Casey dominated the Saddle Bronc event in the 1950s. Was World Champion in that event in 1949, 1951, 1952, 1953, 1954, and 1959. He also was World Champion in Bareback Bronc Riding in 1951. He was All-Around Champion Cowboy in 1951 and again in 1955. 1955 inducted in NRHF. 1979 inducted in PRHF.

Dick Truitt (1904–1978)—Steer Roper, Steer Wrestler, and Calf Roper were the events Dick competed in throughout the 1930s and 1940s. He won many of the major rodeos in these events and he captured the World Championship in Steer Roping in 1939. 1983 inducted in NRHF.

Pancho Villa (1878–1923)—Mexican revolutionary and guerilla leader. After 1914, he engaged in civil war and banditry.

Shoat Webster (1925–2013)—World Champion Steer Roper 1949, 1950, 1954, 1955. 1990 inducted in NRHF. 1979 inducted in PRHF.

George Weir (1918–1989)—World Champion Steer Roper in 1932. Broke horses for the US Calvary during WW1.

George Williams (1932–) Saddle bronco rider and rodeo judge. Editor of Rodeo Sports News 1965–1966, associate editor and publisher of *Persimmon Hill* magazine, and publisher of *The Wild Bunch* magazine at the NCWHM in the 1970s. 2008 inducted in NRHF.

APPENDIX 2
Ike Rude, Historic Ranches, and the Great War
Michael R. Grauer

The Mexican *vaquero* is the direct ancestor of the North American cowboy. Likewise, rodeo (from the Spanish verb *rodear,* meaning "to encircle" or "round up") truly began in Mexico. *Rodeo* remained the preferred term for a "round up" well into the early twentieth century in some parts of the American Southwest, including on ranches where Ike Rude cowboyed. Throwing a looped rope from horseback to catch cattle emerged in the seventeenth century, a technique combining north (horseback) and west (rope) African technologies. "By the middle of the eighteenth century the practice occurred throughout New Spain [Mexico]." German traveler Carl Sartorius described the vaqueros' use of lassos: "They are a peculiar people, simple and hardy, well mounted and excellent riders . . . with a lasso of leather hanging down from the saddle, and with long spurs on their capacious boots." [1]

Initially using a rope required extending the loop on a long pole from horseback with the other end of the rope tied to the horse's tail. By the middle of the 1600s, this technique had been demonstrated in the Plaza of Madrid by "Creole slaves." [2] This "demonstration" may have been the first public performance of "cow work," a type of show that would become rodeo.

The sport of professional rodeo sprang from "cow and horse work" that developed along with the introduction of cattle and horses to North America by 1521, was spurred by the cattle drives after the Civil War, and honed by the end of World War I. On ranches across the Americas, mainly as a result of boredom and isolation, at the end of seasonal roundups and long cattle drives, cowhands from different outfits often challenged each other in matches in saddle-bronc riding, calf roping, and steer throwing, especially in roping. Later, top hands from various ranches competed in local fairs, which evolved into the timed events in rodeo today.

Most early "cow-boys" were Anglo Texans (20–25 percent were either African American, Hispanic, or American Indian, with a few girls disguised as boys). Before the trail drives to Kansas railheads, annual spring and fall roundups on the open ranges required multiple cow outfits to work together to separate their different herds. Ramrods and wagon bosses sought good ropers and cowboys good at "breaking" horses. Some cowboys became specialized "bronc fighters," hiring out to different outfits, and the skills of some ropers became legendary.

Competition between outfits working so closely together evolved naturally on the range.

After the fencing of the Great Plains began about 1881, the large, combined roundups generally ended, but cow and horse work changed very little. With definite boundaries between ranches, competition in standard roping and riding skills increased within outfits themselves, and ranches often challenged other ranches to matches. However, cowboys did not ride "broncs" bareback, wrestle steers, or ride steers or bulls as part of their regular work. These feats of daring gained in popularity as events until they eventually became staples of modern rodeo.

Wild West shows provided opportunities for ridicule among savvy "punchers" who flocked to the performances. However, many cowboys adopted for their own rigs parts of the showy costumes of Wild West performers. Early true rodeos—often called "fairs" or "round-ups"—rarely held the same events as a modern rodeo. Some type of roping match was fairly standard fare. Initially, steers were ridden instead of bulls. Trick roping and riding was common in early rodeos, a holdover from the Wild West shows.

The first rodeo on the Southern Plains and one of the first in Texas was held on Main Street in Canadian, Texas, July 4, 1888. Carl Studer wrote that the first rodeo at Canadian was held primarily to "settle a question of superiority of roping between Ellison Carroll and George Washington," the latter a black cowboy. This match roping included other cowboys; Carroll "won the match by easy odds."[3] Carroll (1862–1942) became known as the master of the steer roping event, and in 1904 at San Antonio, he beat

Clay McGonagill (1879–1921) to become the first acknowledged world champion steer roper. Thirty years after that first rodeo, Julius Caesar Studer (1863–1953), started the Anvil Park Rodeo outside Canadian in 1918, helping give Canadian the moniker "Rodeo Town."

Rodeos on the Southern Plains where Ike Rude was reared did not always hold the same events as today's rodeos. The first rodeo at Canadian, for example, had a "joust" with groups of cowboys with "Olde English" team names. A "wild horse race" was often a staple at early rodeos. After the 1888 rodeo at Canadian, nearly every town of any size in the American West attempted to remain connected to its ranching history by sponsoring rodeos between the years 1915 and 1940. Still, the foundation of rodeo remains connected to the jobs of work of vaqueros, drovers, and cowhands from the sixteenth century forward: cow and horse work.

As a cowboy and ranch hand for many years, Ike Rude cowboyed for five of the most storied ranches in the American West.

MILL IRON RANCH, TEXAS

Teenaged Ike Rude worked for the Mill Irons part-time in 1910 when he was in the eighth grade, and full time the winter of 1910–1911.

Established in 1881 in the "lower Panhandle of Texas," namely in parts of Hall, Childress, Motley, and Cottle counties, the Mill Iron Ranch "contained much land that could not be tilled, probably fifty per cent was considered unfit for farming."[4] Childress County abutted then-Greer County, Texas, to the east, so the Mill Irons were fairly close to Ike Rude's home near Mangum, Oklahoma. The Mill Iron range joined the OX and Shoe Nail ranches on the east, the Shoe Bars and Diamond Tails on the north, the F range to the west, and the Matadors to the south.

The Continental Cattle Company established the Mill Iron Ranch in 1881 with William Edgar Hughes (1840–1918) as president, John N. Simpson (1845–1920) as vice president, John W. Buster as general manager, and S. W. Buster as secretary. In 1884, the Continental Cattle Company reorganized with Hughes as president of the new Continental Land and Cattle Company with its main office in St. Louis. The Mill Irons "encouraged settlers to file . . . on school lands in their range" and "furnished the money for filing fees and taxes and other expenses." After the land had been proved up, they "bought" the land from the nesters or exchanged it for land "on the edge of [their] holdings" that "was smooth and productive." After the homestead filing laws changed to allow the filing on four sections, the Mill Irons "grew more rapidly."[5] In 1896 the Mill Irons bought out the adjoining 152,320-acre Rocking Chair Ranch, thus extending its holdings into Collingsworth and Wheeler counties. The Mill Irons also maintained pastures in Montana.

The Mill Irons followed the axiom coined by cattleman S. P. Britt of Shamrock, Texas, that "the only way to make a ranch pay is to use dugouts and chuckwagons for headquarters" as it "is headquarters that eat up the profit." All line camps were dugouts until headquarters were built south of Estelline, Texas, at Well 62 in 1887. When it burned in 1897, headquarters was moved into Estelline, where Hughes built a house nearby for his use during trips down from Denver.

The Mill Irons brand allegedly originated when a cowboy working for Simpson near Bitter Lake on the Pease River found a maverick and branded it with an iron from a nearby mill. Simpson used the brand on his small herd of cattle; when he sold the cattle and brand to the Continental Cattle Company, the Mill Iron became its official brand.

During its heyday, the Mill Irons branded between 10,000 and 12,000 calves annually. At the 1890 roundup the cattle herd tallied at 30,000 head, and by the 1898 roundup the tally raised to 50,000. They shipped about 4,000 head per year. The Mill Irons became known as a "straight, honest ranch, pleasant to deal with" and "always attended to their own business, and let others alone, always branded their own stock and did not get confused as to the ownership of stray cattle."[6]

The Mill Irons branded differently than other ranches in the region. Penning mother cow and calf together, they "used no rope to catch the calf." Instead, they bulldogged the calves. They were reputed to brand 400 to 600 calves in a day.[7]

The Mill Irons held the reputation for having the largest roundups and the longest drives of any Texas Panhandle ranch. Although most Texas Panhandle cattlemen stopped driving their cattle to market and stockers to northern ranges after the arrival of the railroads by 1888, the Mill Irons continued driving on the Western Trail until 1896 even though the drovers often had to make long detours around homesteaders in Kansas on the Western Trail. In 1894 the Mill Irons drove two-year-old steers to

Montana, then two years later they drove horses from their Montana horse ranch to Texas "for use on the ranch or for sale to settlers." The Mill Irons became known for their "big, bony horses." Hands selected smaller horses for ranch work and traded the larger ones to nesters as the "wiry Spanish 'willowtails' . . . were better suited to ranch work."[8]

Sadly, Mill Iron horses played leading roles in one of the great tragedies on the range. In the late 1890s, glanders disease struck their horse herd. Thirty-five horses were driven into Brewster Canyon and shot. The Mill Iron "boys refused to take part in the killing," as it seemed the veterinarian diagnosed the malady in "their favorite, their warm friend among all their string, which was sentenced" to be destroyed.

The Mill Irons also held on to their longhorn stock long after the neighboring ranches had "bred off the horn and built up the blood." In 1898 they bought two thousand JA grade (bred up) cattle and a thousand JJ full-blood Herefords. They kept their bulls in two separate, heavily fenced pastures on the east and west sides of the ranch. Mill Irons cow puncher James D. Vardy gave a vivid description of the hazards of gathering these bulls in the fall, some to be shipped to market:

> When gathering old bulls we would go several miles from camp, scatter out in bunches, three, four, or five men in a bunch and turn back toward camp and when we found one we started him toward camp. If he showed a disposition not to want to go, which they most always did, we were provided with a what we called a prod pole . . . We would do up our rope as if we were preparing to rope, hold our prod pole in our right hand, and lope up near enough to his side to throw our prod into him. We were always careful not to get close enough for him to gore our horses . . . The best place to impress him with the importance of going in was to throw your spear into his ribs or shoulder blade, which was hard to get loose from. Did you say pitch and bawl? They did both. We surely enjoyed it. It was equal to a rodeo.[9]

Shipping cattle by rail became more economical and the cattle arrived at their destination in better condition. The Mill Irons shipped primarily from Clarendon, Childress, Estelline, and Giles. Estelline became one of the largest cattle shipping points on the Fort Worth and Denver City Railway. Other ranches that shipped from Estelline included the Matadors,

Pitchforks, Shoe Nails, the F, and SMS (Swenson). Sometimes herds driven to Estelline had to wait a week or more to ship. Cowboys rode night and day to prevent intermingling with cattle from other ranches.[10]

In addition to being known for having "the largest horses and the largest men," the Mill Irons was said to employ hands who "enjoyed rough horse-play so much that cowboys often actually dreaded working for the ranch." The long-time wagon boss, Bill Taylor, "made life difficult for the boys who came to help at roundup time." Roundups often used seasonal hands who worked other non-cowboy jobs during the rest of the year. Taylor or some of the other "oversized men who worked under him" never ceased playing practical jokes on "some outside man or new hand." During spring roundup "no one slept a whole night through" for a full week after the wagon pulled out. Ike Rude was small, a "new hand," and only a teenager when he worked for the Mill Irons.

The Mill Irons began reducing their range in 1913. Clarendon cattleman Will Lewis leased a hundred thousand acres that year and ran his Spur cattle on it. The Crews brothers purchased the Rocking Chair Range soon after. In March 1916 Hughes became president of the W. E. Hughes and Company and in October of the same year Hughes became sole owner of the ranch. Over the years, the original range of the Mill Iron contracted to 30,000 acres in Collingsworth County. The Hughes family ran the ranch until 2003, when they sold it to the Allred family, which still operates the ranch as a cow-calf operation.[11]

However, as Laura Hamner wrote, perhaps the most remarkable "feature of the Mill Iron was the occasional visits of the owner," Colonel Hughes. Although he had arrived at what would become the Mill Iron range in the early 1880s driving a "huge, bright-colored Concord coach, drawn by six bobtailed English horses," and lost the coach to quicksand in the Salt Fork of the Red River, he was not long despondent over the loss. He loved to drive a coach-and-six, and bought others. Neither the cowhands nor the nesters envied him; "they merely marveled at and enjoyed him" as he "dashed about the several counties in which his holdings lay." Hughes manipulated the traces of a "satin-smooth" team of six horses, "driving a large coach with gay trappings." He would doff his hat and bow low to all those he passed, as his rounds "took on the dignity and pomp of a royal progress."[12]

6666 RANCH, TEXAS

Although Ike Rude never worked for the 6666s, Tom Burnett (1871–1938) offered him a job there after he left the Mill Irons. Furthermore, Ike got his start in roping as a full-time career at a 1921 roping on the 6666 ranch at Iowa Park, Texas. At this roping, he beat all the tough ropers in the area and established his reputation as one of the finest ropers in the country. His friendship with Tom Burnett continued until Tom's death in 1938, with Ike often stopping to see Tom whenever his travels would take him close to the 6666s.

In 1858, after moving with his family from Missouri to Denton County, Texas, Samuel Burk Burnett (1849–1922), father of Tom Burnett, went into the cattle business for himself in 1870. He purchased 100 head wearing the 6666 brand from Frank Crowley of Denton. After grazing over 1,100 steers near Wichita, Kansas, through the winter of 1873, he sold the cattle for a $10,000 profit. In 1881 he established his headquarters near today's Wichita Falls, Texas.

Burnett negotiated a 300,000-acre grass lease with Comanche Chief Quanah Parker (1845–1911) on the Kiowa-Comanche-Apache Reservation in southwestern Indian Territory. In 1898 the lease was discontinued by the federal government to open Oklahoma Territory for settlement. Burnett traveled to Washington, DC, where he met with President Theodore Roosevelt, who gave him a two-year extension on the lease to find new ranges for his cattle.

Between 1900 and 1903 Burnett purchased 107,520 acres in Carson County northeast of Amarillo, Texas, and bought the Old "8" Ranch, of 141,000 acres, near Guthrie, Texas, in King County, east of Lubbock, Texas. He built the 6666 Supply House and a new headquarters at Guthrie.

Burk Burnett leased the ranchlands to his only son, Tom Burnett, in 1910. Starting as a ranch hand, Tom learned the cattle business in the 1880s in Indian Territory in the Wichita Mountains. He worked as a wagon hand in the Comanche-Kiowa Reservation, drawing the same wages as other cowboys, as well as a line rider. About 1890 his father made him wagon boss of the Nation (Indian Territory) wagon. Also in 1910, he acquired the 26,000 acre Triangle Ranch at Iowa Park, Texas, and in 1912 he inherited one-fourth of his grandfather's Wichita County properties and a large sum of money. Oil discoveries in the county further enlarged his fortune.

Tom Burnett built his own cattle empire and when he died, his Triangle and the trusteeship of his father's 6666 passed to Tom's only daughter, Anne Valliant Burnett Tandy (1900–1980). "Miss Anne" oversaw the Triangles and 6666s, and helped found the American Quarter Horse Association. At her passing in 1980 the 6666s and the Triangles went to her daughter, Anne Burnett Windfohr Marion (1938–2020). "Little Anne" sold the Triangle and focused on the 6666s. At her passing in 2020, the Burnett Ranches encompassed 260,000 acres, including the 6666 Ranch headquarters near Guthrie and the Dixon Creek Ranch between Panhandle and Borger, Texas.

In January 2022, Taylor Sheridan, who writes, produces, and acts in the hit television show *Yellowstone*, is at the helm of the group that purchased the 6666 Ranch.

MATADOR RANCH, TEXAS AND MONTANA

Ike Rude worked on the Matador Ranch from 1911 to 1914.

Confederate veteran and Texan Henry H. "Hank" Campbell (1840–1911) drove a herd into the Tongue River range in today's Motley County, Texas, in 1879. Having already trailed herds to Dodge City, New Orleans, and Nevada, he took another to Chicago in 1878, where he grossed fourteen dollars per head. Invited to a luncheon by Chicago bankers, including Colonel Alfred Markham Britton, Campbell agreed to "secure land in the western part of his state [Texas], stock the range through the Colonel's financing, and manage the ranch."[13] The other partners included Spottswood W. Lomax and John W. Nichols, both of Fort Worth, and a Mr. Cata, a brother-in-law of Colonel Britton from New York. As "an enthusiast of Spanish literature," Lomax gave the ranching venture its name: Matador. When Lomax and Britton partnered again in 1883 to organize another ranch, Lomax dubbed it the Espuela (Spur) Cattle Company.

The first cattle on the Matador Cattle Company range came from South Texas in December 1879 and were branded "V." This became known as the famous "Matador V." Campbell also acquired smaller herds in 1880 and 1881, including cattle with John Chisum's Jingle Bob earmark. By custom the purchaser received the grazing and watering rights from the seller on the fenceless ranges. By 1882 the Matadors claimed a million and a half acres with one hundred thousand acres fronting water.

Campbell built a two-room house at Ballard Springs with lumber hauled from Fort Griffin and window frames from Fort Worth that came

married in 1867. They divided their time between America and their estates in England and Ireland.

In the fall of 1874, the Adairs took a hunting trip in western Nebraska in the company of a military escort from Sidney Barracks. The Adair party traveled via the Union Pacific Railroad from Omaha. Fifty US cavalrymen under the command of Colonel Richard Irving Dodge led the hunting party to the South Platte River, where they set up camp near a Sioux village. During a chase after buffalo, John Adair shot his horse in the head, killing it and slightly injuring himself. They returned to New York via Cheyenne, Wyoming; Denver, Central City, and Colorado Springs, Colorado; and St. Louis. This hunting trip "caused [the Adairs] to become interested in the West and they determined to return next year [1875] and acquire a large tract of land. John Adair moved his brokerage from New York to Denver where he met Goodnight in 1876.[26]

Goodnight purchased one hundred head of the best Durham bulls in Colorado to improve the herd in the Palo Duro. Adair and his wife, and Goodnight and his wife, Mary Ann Dyer Goodnight (1839–1926), outfitted themselves in Trinidad, Colorado, with four wagons, six months of supplies and equipment, and a light ambulance. Two cowboys accompanied the party, "who made much fun of the fact that they were starting a ranch with a herd of bulls." Cornelia Adair, an accomplished horsewoman, rode the entire way (about three hundred miles) and Molly Goodnight drove one of the wagon teams.

Goodnight and his crew built the "Old Home Ranch" headquarters from large native cedars in the canyon bottom in today's Armstrong County, Texas. Their partnership became official on June 18, 1877, and would last five years. At Goodnight's suggestion, the ranch used Adair's initials: a connected J and A. Goodnight received a $2,500 salary to manage the ranch. After five years, the proceeds of the operation would be divided, with two-thirds to Adair and one-third to Goodnight.[27]

Initially supplied by ox teams from Trinidad, Colorado, by 1880 the JAs were contracted with Lee and Reynolds, sutlers at Fort Elliott. Ten drivers with thirty wagons brought "six months supplies for fifty men, corn for a hundred horses, and sixty-seven miles of barbed wire" from Dodge City. In 1882, the Fort Worth & Denver City Railway reached Wichita Falls, Texas, and the JAs were supplied from there.

Goodnight drove the first JA trail herd to Dodge City, Kansas—then the nearest railhead—in 1878. In 1879, Goodnight moved the JA headquarters east into Donley County, building a house of cedar logs that still stands as of 2023 as the second-oldest surviving ranch house in the Texas Panhandle, after the T Anchor Ranch house built in 1877.

As manager of the JA, Goodnight improved JA cattle by bringing in European cattle. He bought two hundred head of registered Shorthorn bulls and three hundred heifers at Burlingame, Kansas, from O. H. "Bull" Nelson (1850–1930) in the spring of 1881. After being shipped to Dodge City, these Shorthorns were driven to the JA Ranch. Then in 1883, Goodnight bought from Nelson about 1,050 head of Hereford bulls, cows, and calves, and established the recognized quality of the JA's Hereford herd. Goodnight built one of the Panhandle's first barbed wire fences in 1882. Goodnight also kept a herd of buffalo (American bison) and cross-bred some with cattle to create "cattalo." He later maintained a wildlife park with buffalo, elk, deer, and pronghorns near his home at Goodnight, allowing some of the buffalo to roam the JA Ranch.

By 1882, the JA Ranch comprised 93,000 acres. By Adair's death in 1885 the ranch used 1,325,000 acres in parts of Randall, Armstrong, Donley, Hall, Briscoe, and Swisher Counties. Goodnight's rules for his cowboys were fairly rigid—just as they were on the Shoe Bars, the XITs, and many ranches west of the 100th meridian: no gambling, no drinking, and no fighting. With the managers of the Spurs and the Matadors, he agreed to not employ any hand "discharged elsewhere for theft or drunkenness." Goodnight and neighboring cattlemen even declared the country south of the North Fork of the Red River to be under a state of "prohibition." For, while the owners and managers "relished the qualities of good cocktails themselves . . . they realized that whiskey, cards, and cows mix but poorly."[28] Ironically, Goodnight fired his own brother-in-law, Walter Dyer, and demoted James W. ("Jack") Ritchie (1861–1924), Cornelia Adair's son by her first marriage, after catching them drunk and gambling in Clarendon and at the headquarters of the Tule Ranch division in late 1887.

Although a naturalized British citizen who spent most of her time in Ireland, Cornelia Adair also maintained a home in Clarendon and visited the JA regularly. She contributed generously to various civic projects, including funds to build the Adair hospital (largely devoted to cowboy healthcare) and the first YMCA building in Clarendon, and strongly supported that community's Episcopal church. Cornelia Adair continued the partnership with Goodnight until 1888, who received the Quitaque division as his own. Goodnight had purchased the Quitaque division in Briscoe County, Texas, for Cornelia Adair in 1882 and fenced it the following year.

John E. Farrington succeeded Goodnight for three years, from 1887 to 1890. Then, under the management of Richard "Dick" Walsh (?–1921) from 1892 to 1910, the JA herd became one of the finest quality herds of cattle in the United States.[29] Walsh came to the JAs in 1885 from Ireland and, starting at "the lowest round of the ladder, he passed through the various phases of ranch work, until he was fully equipped for the responsible managerial position."[30]

Jarrett William Kent (1883–1945) began cowboying for the JA Ranch in 1883, worked as wagon boss for the Tule division, then became range boss, and was superintendent from 1911 to 1927. During the 1930s he worked as assistant superintendent. Kent had lost his foot due to a hay wagon accident and had a wooden foot. The JA blacksmith probably built him a hand-forged special stirrup to lock his wooden foot in place while on horseback. Ike Rude worked under Kent, who took a great interest in his roping career.

Kent and the wagon boss would set the date for the annual spring roundup, usually between the first and tenth of May, depending on when the "grass [would] furnish good grazing for the horses." The day and night before the chuck wagon set out, the JAs held a "big dinner and *baile* [dance]." The cowboys were all given a holiday the day before the dinner and baile, and most went to town (probably Clarendon or Claude) to get his "'hair cut off' (haircut) and his 'whiskers drove in' (shave)" and to make "a date with his best girl."[31]

After dinner at 5 o'clock, preparations began for the all-night dance, which started about 6:30 pm and was held in the bunk room at the bunkhouse. Some of the "JA boys" provided the music on fiddle, guitar, and banjo, although in 1927 the ensemble included a saxophone. Famed early Western music star Eck Robertson performed on the fiddle at this dance before he recorded what some consider the first "country" music commercial record in 1922.[32] Among the tunes were "Arkansas Traveler," "Turkey in the Straw," "Ragtime Annie," and "Casey Jones." Two cowboys acted as "floor managers," and about every sixth dance was an "old-fashioned square dance." A "city smart aleck" often showed up uninvited and attempted to show the cowboys "the modern way of dancing, much to the disgust of the cowboys." The dance continued until midnight, when a lunch was served of sandwiches, fruit salad, and coffee. The dance resumed until daybreak, when "Home Sweet Home" was played and the festivities concluded. The guests left and the cowboys prepared to leave with the chuck wagon at sunup.

The JAs divided their roundup crews into hands doing "flat work" and "canyon work." The roundup lasted about six to seven weeks in both the spring and fall, with the canyon work taking slightly longer than the flat work due to the terrain. After rising as early as 3 am, cowboys often rode ten miles from the chuck wagon into the rough breaks of the canyons for the day's work. Canyon work usually involved the rounding up of "outlaws" or old cattle that had been missed for years in previous roundups and became quite wild. These "mossy horns" provided "harder work and more excitement than the average calf." Canyon work also required the pushing of yearling steers and shipper cattle down into flatter pastures. The hands called these herds "windies" due to the warm weather at that time of year, the contrariness of the cattle, and the difficulty in driving them out of the breaks, gullies, and arroyos. Thus, the cattle, horses, and cowboys were all "winded" by the time all were out on the flats. After the spring round-up the cowboys were usually given three days off to celebrate Independence Day.

The cook awakened the hands about 3:30 to 4 am, and after catching and saddling their horses and having a cup of coffee and a cigarette, work began. Horses were usually "green broke," and "tenderfeet" often saw their horse "running with the stirrups . . . shaking hands above the horse's back" after every jump. The tenderfoot typically rode a "new full-stamped saddle," which squeaked or creaked while the horse pitched, whereas the "old hand seldom gets thrown off, and seldom has a saddle with any stamping." Moreover, the old hand's saddle was "an old one with all the squeak ridden out of it."[33] Typically a cowboy had six to seven horses in his "string." Around mid-day, cowboys ate a dinner usually of sourdough biscuits, frijoles, and beef, caught a new horse, and started in again.

Generally, spring roundups involved branding calves and gathering fat calves, yearling steers, and heifers for shipment and delivery. Fall roundups focused on the gathering of beef cattle for shipping, feeding, or stocking other ranges, and the separation of mama cows from their calves. Fall roundups also included the gather and selecting of young horses to be broken for cow work. Winter work involved being assigned to a line camp with a lone cowboy living and working on a section of the ranch alone. Tom Blasingame (1898–1989), for example, lived at the Campbell Creek camp alone for most of his seventy-three years on the JAs, from 1916 until 1989, except for the two years he worked for the Double Circles in Arizona. The camp had no electricity and no telephone; and after 1933 he would return to Claude on weekends to be with his wife, Eleanor.

At Cornelia Adair's death in 1921, she left the bulk of the JA properties to "Jack" Ritchie, her son from her first marriage, and his heirs. T. D. Hobart (1855–1935) became the JA manager in 1915, an executor of the estate of Cornelia Adair in 1921, and became sole administrator of the JA Ranch in 1932.

By 1928, the JA Ranch comprised 397,800 acres (622 sections), divided into forty-eight pastures of varying sizes. The ranch included parts of Armstrong, Briscoe, Donley, and Hall Counties in Texas. Twelve winter or line camps are scattered across the JAs where a cowboy's family, or a lone cowboy, lived throughout the year. The ranch also had five farms on which "feedstuff" was raised as well as some cotton on some of them. [34]

In 1935, Montgomery H. W. ("Monte") Ritchie (1910–1999), Cornelia's grandson, took over as manager. Ten years later the JA held 335,000 acres in Armstrong, Briscoe, Donley, and Hall Counties. In 1960 the house was designated a national historic landmark. Noted for its purebred Herefords and Angus bulls and its registered Quarter Horses, the JA Ranch lent a herd of Texas longhorns to Palo Duro Canyon State Park. The ranch also gave its historic bison herd to Caprock Canyons State Park near Quitaque.

Among the JA cowboys whom Ike Rude befriended was Henry Rowden (1888–1966), who began working for the JAs in 1907. Rude and Rowden surely had some adventures together. Ike Rude may have witnessed a shootout on the JAs in June 1920 in which another cowboy, Jack Woods, attempted to kill Henry Rowden by firing a Winchester rifle at him. Woods's bullet hit Henry's saddle horn, blasting fragments into his face and arm. He returned fire once with a revolver, but the other cowboys intervened before more bullets could fly. Both men were arrested and indicted for "assault with attempt to murder" in Armstrong County, Texas. Both were acquitted. Henry Rowden later worked for both the Chiricahuas and Double Circles as well, before returning to the JAs.

CHIRICAHUA CATTLE COMPANY, ARIZONA

Ike Rude worked on the Chiricahuas from 1915 to 1916.

One of two major ranches in Cochise County, Arizona, initiated by Pennsylvanians, the Chiricahua Cattle Company (CCC) incorporated in 1885. The other was the Erie Cattle Company, formed in 1883. Comprised of several smaller outfits, some founded as early as 1877, the CCC's combined water and property rights included 1.6 million acres of grazing land. The CCCs became one of Arizona's largest range-cattle ranches in the area of southeastern Arizona that was formerly occupied by Apaches.[35]

The consolidation of eight small ranches in the north end of Sulphur Spring Valley in southeastern Arizona in 1885 created a range seventy-five miles long and thirty-five miles wide called the Chiricahua Cattle Company. Three brothers, Theodore, Thomas, and Jarrett White established the El Dorado Ranch on Turkey Creek in 1877. Thomas and Jarrett sold out to John V. Vickers in 1883. Thomas White established another ranch on the San Pedro River; Theodore and Jarrett created the Cochise Hardware and Trading Company at Tombstone. John Vickers acted as a livestock commission agent for the area's small ranchers at fifty cents per animal. In April 1885, Theodore White convinced his neighboring ranchers to pool their assets into the Chiricahua Cattle Company with the CCC brand registered in Cochise County.[36]

The Tombstone Stock Growers Association, or Cochise County Livestock Association, was conceived of in spring 1885 to "control rustling, police the range, and simplify roundups." The association drafted regulations for "assembly of cattle, the handling of mavericks or stray calves . . . and the conduct of roundup participants." The association divided the county into three roundup districts for each spring and fall roundup. Ranchers in each district designated "the time and place of their respective rodeos, as roundups were then called." The district's ranchers also selected a "Judge of the Plains," so named by territorial statute. This "boss of the plains" directed the jobs of work during the rodeo, settled disputes over ownership, and the "bad conduct of participants." The association also levied a 2.5-cent "tax" per animal rounded up to its members. Ineffective registration and duplication of brands lead to the appointment of brand inspectors. The association also pushed the territorial legislature for stronger laws against cattle rustling.

The Tombstone Stock Growers Association also defied exorbitant freight rates by the Southern Pacific Railroad. In 1889 they drove herds to Deming, New Mexico, for shipment over the Santa Fe Railroad line to the east. The following year, Cochise County cattlemen drove their herds to California. Finally, in March 1891, "sixteen vaqueros supervised by Pete Johnson, 'an old trail man,'" planned to drive 2,000 head across New Mexico and the Texas Panhandle to ranges south of Dodge City. When the herd reached Deming, the Santa Fe made concessions that forced the hand of the Southern Pacific, and the railroad capitulated.[37]

An 1892 US Army contract to supply 900,000 pounds of beef annually to the White Mountain and San Carlos Apache reservations awarded to the CCCs resulted in a need for financial capital. The First National Bank of Los Angeles sold bonds on the company that allowed it to replace livestock and search for pastures in other states. Vickers partnered with Walter Vail of the Empire Ranch (straddling Pima and Cochise Counties), and Carroll W. Gates (who also partnered with Vail on grazing leases for the Empire in southern California and on the Turkey Track ranch in Arizona). Vickers, Vail, and Gates purchased 14,000 acres in Sherman County, Texas, and Beaver County, Indian Territory, respectively, in 1894 for a feeder operation called the Panhandle Pasture Company. Vail and Gates also acquired a half-interest in the CCCs by mid-March 1894.[38]

By the fall of 1897, the Chiricahua Cattle Company had culled 17,000 head of its inferior cattle, sending a few one- and two-year olds to the Panhandle Pasture Company. The CCCs converted their Sulphur Spring Valley operations to be used purely for breeding. They brought in Hereford bulls from cattle buyer/seller Henry S. Boice with connections to Gudgell and Simpson of Independence, Missouri, "the greatest Hereford breeding establishment in America."[39] Theodore White and John Vickers helmed the CCCs boldly. However, by March 1898, White had divested himself of his shares in the company. And "southeastern Arizona's range cattle industry began to unravel."

Free grazing on public domain lands had ended. Homesteaders had claimed tracts in the Sulphur Spring Valley and the ranges were being fenced. John Vickers left Tombstone for Denver became involved in real estate development at Huntington Beach and Long Beach, California, with his brother, Sumner. Yet, John Vickers remained president, and Sumner vice president of the CCCs. However, in 1909 they sold their interests to

Henry Boice and W. T. Johnson, a Kansas City livestock commission agent. Boice and Johnson would drastically alter the Chiricahua Cattle Company and other southeastern Arizona ranches.

The new bosses renamed the CCCs "Boice, Gates, and Johnson." The 1909 Desert Land Act opened the Sulphur Spring Valley to settlers from Oklahoma, Texas, and Kansas. Boice sold off water rights and deeded property. He increased grazing on the San Carlos and White Mountain reservations until the Indian Service discontinued issuing permits to non-Native Americans. At Henry Boice's death in 1919, his son Henry G. Boice became manager and acquired additional range for the 20,000 head of cattle (which some called "Cherry Cows," a corruption of the name "Chiricahua"). By 1945, Charles Boice had liquidated all the former Chiricahua Cattle Company ranches.[40]

DOUBLE CIRCLES, ARIZONA

Ike Rude, Tom Blasingame, and Henry Rowden all cowboyed for the Double Circles.

Railroad owner Colonel Joseph H. Hampson founded the Double Circles in 1883 when he purchased a small sheep spread on Eagle Creek from George H. Stevens, a former agent and trader at the San Carlos Apache Reservation.[41] Hampson stocked the new ranch with Texas longhorns, and expanded the Double Circle Ranch to eventually numbere over 700,000 acres.[42] After Hampson's death, the ranch passed to the Drumm Cattle Commission Company of Kansas City. Later, George and Asa Jones of Marfa, Texas, and Joe Espy of Alpine, Texas, owned the Double Circles when the Coolidge Dam was built on the San Carlos Apache Reservation between 1924 and 1928. These ranchers sold the ranch to the US government, who turned it over to the Apaches in 1932.

The Double Circles also provided succor for a notorious outlaw, "Bronco Bill" Walters (1869–1921), and his gang that included William "Kid" Johnson (?–1898) and Daniel "Red" Pipkin (1876–1938). Walters and his confederates had "punch[ed] cows on the Double Circles" and the "cowboys were their friends and they came and went without let or hindrance." The gang kept "two good mounts well-conditioned on Double Circle oats" and "came [there] for refuge in 1898."[43] After attempting to rob a Santa Fe Railroad train west of Gallup, New Mexico Territory, a posse chased them onto the

Double Circles range. Johnson and Walters ambushed the posse and rode on to ranch headquarters at Eagle Creek. After another Santa Fe Railway robbery of a Wells Fargo safe near Belen, Sheriff Francisco Vigil and his deputy Daniel Bustamante of Los Lunas pursued them to Alamosa Creek, where both lawmen were killed and Johnson was shot. The gang returned to the Double Circles to heal and hole up.

Acting as an agent for Wells Fargo, famed lawman Jeff Milton (1861–1947), in partnership with another famous lawman, George Scarborough (1859–1900), Eugene Thacker, and a Diamond A cowboy named Martin, tracked Bronco Bill and his gang to a Double Circles horse corral camp on the Black River in the White Mountains.

J. Evetts Haley wrote that Milton cowboyed for the Double Circles as part of his undercover work for the Central New Mexico Stock Association in the late 1880s.[44] Milton worked as a Texas Ranger primarily in the Trans Pecos and Big Bend areas as the Southern Pacific Railroad laid new track into El Paso. He later became a small rancher in New Mexico Territory, where he also worked as a deputy sheriff and a cattle detective tracking rustlers. In 1887 he became a US Customs agent riding from El Paso to the Gulf of California. In 1894 as the new El Paso Chief of Police, Milton faced down and disarmed the infamous John Wesley Hardin. He was quoted as saying, "I never killed a man who didn't need killing and I never shot an animal except for meat."

After arresting eight Double Circles cowboys and a bear hunter at the Black River camp, Milton and Scarborough lay in wait. When Bronco Bill, Johnson, and Pipkin rode up unsuspectingly, Milton attempted to arrest them. He shot Bronco Bill in the arm and chest and Johnson through the hips. Milton then likely saved Bronco Bill from drowning in his own blood. Red Pipkin escaped.

Milton and Scarborough sent Double Circles cowboy "Climax Jim" to Fort Apache and Solomonville with one of the most famous lawman's messages in the Old West: "Send a coffin and a doctor." Fearing reprisals from the Double Circles cowhands, the terrified doctor "said 'neither [man] could live'" and, after he "administered some morphine," he returned to the fort with an escort of soldiers. Johnson died that night and was buried there.

Meanwhile, Milton, "knowing he had no friends in the region," arrested and disarmed all who rode up until he had about twenty men impounded in the horse corral. When a deputy sheriff and posse arrived, clearly fearful of the detained men, Milton drove them away with, "Goddamn you, what are you doing here if you ain't our friends? Get out of this camp and get out right now."[45] He splinted and dressed Bronco Bill's wounds and tied him onto the back of a horse for the forty-mile mountain trail ride to Geronimo, Arizona Territory. Milton escorted Bronco Bill by train to Socorro, where the outlaw received a life sentence to the penitentiary at Santa Fe. Pardoned in 1917 after twenty years, he returned to cowboy for the Diamond As where he died from a fall from a windmill tower in 1921.

Meanwhile, Red Pipkin attempted to return to the Double Circles headquarters a month after the gunfight. After threatening the foreman, Joe Terrill, he learned that Bronco Bill's sanctuary on the ranch was no more. Nevertheless, because of its isolation, the Double Circles range remained a place where outlaws could still disappear.

IKE RUDE AND THE GREAT WAR

Cowboys and cowboy imagery played vital roles for the United States and Canada during World War I (1914–1918). The Calgary Exhibition, which became known as the "Khaki Fair," promoted the significance of western agricultural production to the war, while the Stampede served as a training ground. Buffalo Bill partnered with the 101 Ranch Wild West Show in a Pageant of Preparedness that included US cavalry charges and artillery demonstrations. Cowboys from Oregon decorated their US army cannon with "Let 'er Buck!" and the 91st ("Wild West") Division adopted the slogan, "Powder River, Let 'er Buck!"

When American troops debarked in France wearing their distinct campaign hats, French civilians celebrated by noting that the doughboys were wearing "*chapeaus des cowboys*" (cowboy hats); in other words, the Americans—cowboys all in French eyes—had arrived to save the day. And indeed they had.

However, in the American Southwest, another conflict—this time in Mexico—had repercussions on both sides of the border. Ike Rude experienced some of these effects indirectly.

The United States maintained an often-violated official policy of neutrality toward Mexico during the country's revolution of 1910–1920. From April to November 1914, the US navy occupied Veracruz in retaliation for the Tampico Affair. The raid on Norias Ranch and other cross-border actions by revolutionaries led to a tense environment with state guards from

Texas and Oklahoma and Texas Ranger companies deployed along the Rio Grande.

After Venustiano Carranza seized power in Mexico in 1915, the United States supported his government and ceased support of revolutionaries like Pancho Villa. After the lack of American arms and equipment proved disastrous for the Villistas, Villa abandoned traditional warfare and took to the hills of Chihuahua as a guerilla. In retaliation for US support of Carranza, in March 1916, Villa kidnapped and killed eighteen Americans and launched a raid on Columbus, New Mexico, killing eighteen more Americans and burning the town. Villa lost around a hundred men due to the US Army presence.

In retaliation for the raid, President Woodrow Wilson appointed US General John Pershing to lead a "Punitive Expedition" to capture or kill Pancho Villa. Ultimately the raid was unsuccessful, but the process of deploying troops and carrying out a large invasion of hostile territory helped prepare some of the American military for when the US declared war on Germany. They used aircraft, armored cars, and other advanced weaponry for the first time during the Punitive Expedition.

In January 1917, British cryptographers deciphered a telegram from German Foreign Minister Arthur Zimmermann to the German Minister to Mexico, Heinrich von Eckhardt, offering the return to Mexico of territory lost to the US during the Mexican-American War (Texas, New Mexico, Arizona, and California) in return for joining the German cause. The "Zimmerman telegram" prompted the US declaration of war against Germany on April 6, 1917. US interventions caused Mexico to remain neutral throughout the Great War.

Born José Doroteo Arango Arámbula to poor sharecroppers on one of the largest *haciendas* in Durango, Mexico, Francisco "Pancho" Villa (1878–1923) either took the "Villa" name in tribute to his grandfather, Jesús Villa, or he appropriated the name from a Coahuilan bandit. After allegedly defending his younger sister's honor by shooting the offender, Villa became an outlaw, including rustling cattle in Chihuahua. Revolutionaries recruited Villa to fight for Francisco Madero and he became leader of the División del Norte cavalry and eventually governor of Chihuahua. Villa retired in 1920 to his hacienda in Chihuahua but was assassinated in 1923 near Parral, possibly by agents of his rival, General Álvaro Obregón, and Melitón Lozoya, the former owner of Villa's hacienda.

Thirty-six nations fought in the Great War. Over nine million service men and women died directly from the war and there were over thirty-seven million casualties worldwide. More than four million Americans served in the American Expeditionary Force (AEF), with half of those serving overseas. The United States suffered over 350,000 casualties, including 120,000 deaths. Men and women from the American West either volunteered for service in the National Guard, Regular Army, US Marine Corps, or US Navy, or were drafted into the National Army.

Despite not entering the war until 1917, US citizens organized relief efforts almost immediately. President Woodrow Wilson appointed Herbert Hoover director of the newly created Food Administration in May 1917 and the demand for American-produced food greatly increased. Beef and flour poured into Europe from Western North America and agricultural and military production soared. The US also exported thousands of horses and mules to Europe before declaring war in April 1917.

Over eight million horses and mules served in World War I; over 1.3 million came from the United States. Cavalry, artillery, services of supply, and ambulances all used horses and mules. Estimates from the British Broadcasting Company (BBC) put British horses at one million, and a horse advocacy site puts the number of American horses at one million.[46] A British brigadier-general reported in 1918 that "quite two-thirds of the horses and practically all the mules used in the British Army in France and the other theatres of war [came] from the American Continent."[47] Between 1914 and 1917, one thousand horses per day from North America were sent across the Atlantic. Some were mustangs from the US Great Plains states and Canadian provinces and were half wild.[48]

For the American Expeditionary Forces (AEF), poor management of the mobilization of US industry during the lead-up to America's active role in the war contributed to the shortage of horses and mules in France. The lack of space for horses and mules on transport ships directly affected the number of horses and mules (and trucks) accessible to the AEF upon landing in France. By the time the AEF arrived there, the shortage of horses and mules was a serious problem. In July 1917, the French agreed to furnish 7,000 horses and mules per month, but by August informed the US War Department they could not fulfill this contract. Furthermore, obtainable animals had already been rejected by the French army. Early in 1918 by requisition the French government delivered 50,000 animals.[49] After January

West sought a bronze doughboy statue, either E. M. Viquesney's *Spirit of the American Doughboy*, or John Paulding's *American Doughboy*.[62]

In August 1919 Guy Weadick opened the second Calgary Stampede in honor of the end of World War I. Called the "Victory Stampede," all proceeds were promised to the Salvation Army, Great War Veterans' Association, and the YMCA. The souvenir program stated that the show would "demonstrate in typical Western style the joy and exuberance felt here in knowing that the Great War had concluded victoriously for the Allied arms."

Rodeo in the United States got into the act as well with Tex Austin's first Madison Square Garden Championship Rodeo. Proceeds from this show were dedicated to the Argonne Association for the support of French children orphaned in World War I. Legendary rodeo star Bonnie McCarroll captured the Argonne Association trophy in 1922.

Working on ranches in Texas and Arizona and serving in the Great War inured Ike Rude for the grueling schedule that professional rodeo demanded of its competitors. Tempered by unceasing cow and horse work as well as the constant big guns and high explosive shells in France, he was as hardened a cowboy as rodeo would ever see.

—Michael R. Grauer

McCasland Chair of Cowboy Culture/Curator
of Cowboy Collections and Western Art,
National Cowboy and Western Heritage Museum,
Oklahoma City, Oklahoma

NOTES

Introduction

1. Dave Stout, *Rodeo History,* ProRodeo Hall of Fame Publication, April 19, 1976.

2. Willard H. Porter, "Steer Jerkin," *Quarter Horse Journal* 1, no. 11 (August 1949): 4–5.

Chapter 1

1. "Pioneer Stagecoach Stand Operators Mr. and Mrs. Isaac J. Rude," Texas State Historical Marker, Stopping Points, last updated July 15, 2008, https://www.stopping-points.com/texas/sights.cgi?marker=Pioneer+Stagecoach+Stand+Operator +Mr.+and +Mrs.+Isaac+J.+Rude&cnty=pecos.

Chapter 2

1. George Williams, "Rodeo's Iron Man," Persimmon Hill 5, no. 4 (1976): 49–50.

2. Most of this history taken from Professor Charles Townsend, "Taped Interview with Ike Rude," Texas Tech University Oral History Project, August 14, 1969, http://oralhistory.swco.ttu.edu/index.php?title=Rude,_Ike_1969–08–14,_15.

Chapter 3

1. Professor Charles Townsend, "Taped Interview with Ike Rude," Texas Tech University Oral History Project, August 14, 1969, http://oralhistory.swco.ttu.edu/index .php?title=Rude,_Ike_1969–08–14,_15.

Chapter 4

1. This is discussed elsewhere by Michael Grauer in his contribution to this book, Appendix 2, "Ike Rude, Historic Ranches, and the Great War."

2. Willard H. Porter, "The Cowboy They Named a Street For," Frontier Times 53, no. 6 (Oct.– Nov. 1979): 16.

3. Ibid., 40.

4. "Tom Blasingame," Ranches.org, accessed January 6, 2022, http://www.ranches .org/tom_blasingame.htm.

5. Most of the history taken from Professor Charles Townsend, "Taped Interview with Ike Rude," Texas Tech University Oral History Project, August 14, 1969, http://oralhistory.swco.ttu.edu/index.php?title=Rude,_Ike_1969–08–14,_15.

Chapter 5

1. George Williams, "Rodeo's Iron Man," Persimmon Hill 5, no. 4 (1976): 50–51.

2. This quote was taken from Cowboys in Khaki: Westerners in the Great War, exhibition text, National Cowboy and Western Heritage Museum, Oklahoma City, Oklahoma, November 17, 2018, to May 12, 2019.

Chapter 6

1. Jack Moreman, "Jack Moreman: The Stranger, the Old Buffalo and Ike Rude at the JA Ranch," interview by Dusty Reins, Dusty Reins Stories, January 14, 2019, video, 10:28, https://www.youtube.com/watch?v=_Y9gWEBjQLo. Jack Moreman was the JA Ranch manager in the early 1970s.

2. Willard H. Porter, "A Visit with Ike Rude," Quarter Horse Journal (November 1973): 48.

3. Most of the history taken from Professor Charles Townsend, "Taped Interview with Ike Rude," Texas Tech University Oral History Project, August 14, 1969, http://oralhistory.swco.ttu.edu/index.php?title=Rude,_Ike_1969–08–14, 15.

Chapter 7

1. George Williams, "Rodeo's Iron Man," Persimmon Hill 5, no. 4 (1976): 53.

2. Bill King, "On the Road with the Knights of Columbus Rodeo," (1924) article he wrote and attached to a letter to Ike Rude, dated 1977, from family archives.

3. "Ike Rude Is Winner," East Oregonian, August 29, 1931.

4. Williams, "Rodeo's Iron Man," 53.

Chapter 8

1. Frank G. Evans, "Rodeo Stars Take West to Montreal, Sail for London," Fort Worth Star Telegram, May 25, 1934.

2. Willard H. Porter, "A Visit with Ike Rude," Quarter Horse Journal (November 1973): 48.

3. Daily Herald, July 14, 1934, Ike Rude scrapbook, family archives.

4. Hugh L. Bennett, Horseman, Brand of a Legend (Denver: Type-Smith of Colorado, 1992), 185.

Chapter 9

1. Willard H. Porter, 13 Flat (South Brunswick, NJ: A. S. Barnes and Co., Inc., 1967), 164.

2. LaJeanne T. Gilmer, "Wyoming's King in the Hall of Fame," Old West Magazine (Spring 1990) 20, 21.

3. Hugh L. Bennett, Horseman, Brand of a Legend, (Denver: Type-Smith of Colorado,1992), 73–75.

Chapter 11

1. Bruce Beckmann, "Ol' Baldy," America's Horse, a publication for the American Quarter Horse Association's members (July–August 2002): 53.
2. Ibid.
3. Corbett Mason, "Ike Rude," Ronald S. Mason's Cross J Ranch Oklahoma Star & Beggar Boy Rodeo Greats (self-pub., 2020).
4. Willard H. Porter, Roping and Riding (South Brunswick: A. S. Barnes and Co., 1975), 45
5. Ibid., 46.

Chapter 12

1. "Ike Couldn't Bust Loping Longhorn," clipping from unidentified Cheyenne, Wyoming, newspaper, July 29, 1943, Ike Rude scrapbook.

Chapter 13

1. Veterans of Foreign Wars, poster, San Angelo, Texas, 1947.
2. George Williams, "Rodeo's Iron Man," Persimmon Hill 5, no. 4 (1976): 55.
3. Willard H. Porter, 13 Flat (South Brunswick, NJ: A. S. Barnes and Co., Inc., 1967), 164.
4. Ibid., 164.
5. Ike's version of Gail Gardner's "The Sierry Petes," 1917. A very popular poem among cowboys, it can be found in various iterations online, in print, and in memory. I have no record of where or when Ike first learned the version he loved to recite. According to Blake Allmendinger, the first publication approved by the author was in Gail Gardner's 1935 volume Orejana Bull. Allmendinger, The Cowboy: Representations of Labor in an American Work Culture (Oxford: Oxford University Press, 1992), 37.

Chapter 16

1. Tommy Blasingame, "Ike Rude and Heelfly," Tales from Tommy, clipping from unknown magazine, from Ike Rude scrapbook.

Chapter 18

1. Rodeo Historical Society, Extra 1, no. 18.
2. Professor Charles Townsend, "Taped Interview with Ike Rude," Texas Tech University Oral History Project, August 14, 1969, http://oralhistory.swco.ttu.edu/index.php?title=Rude,_Ike_1969–08–14,_15.
3. Sheila Samples, "Rodeo Pioneer," Oklahoma Today (Summer 1983): 31.

4. Zeke Scher, "Is 77 Too Old for a Rodeo Cowboy, Not If Your Name is Ike Rude," Sunday Empire, the magazine of the Denver Post, July 18, 1971, 12–16.

Chapter 21

1. Willard H. Porter, "A Visit with Ike Rude," Quarter Horse Journal (November 1973): 47.

Appendix2

1. Andrew Sluyter, *Black Ranching Frontiers: African Cattle Herders of the Atlantic World, 1500–1900* (New Haven and London: Yale University Press, 2012), 51.

2. Ibid., 53.

3. Carl L. Studer, "The First Rodeo in Texas," *Southwestern Historical Quarterly* 48, no. 3 (January 1945): 372.

4. Lee Gilmore, "The Mill Iron Ranch," *Panhandle-Plains Historical Review* V (1932): 65.

5. Laura V. Hamner, *Short Grass & Longhorns* (Norman: University of Oklahoma Press, 1943), 189–90.

6. Ibid., 190.

7. Ibid., 194.

8. Ibid., 191.

9. James D. Vardy, "Reminiscences," Panhandle-Plains Historical Museum Research Center, Canyon, TX. As cited in Gilmore, "The Mill Iron Ranch," 60–61.

10. Gilmore, "The Mill Iron Ranch," 62.

11. See the Mill Iron Ranches, website, accessed January 15, 2022, www.millironranch .com.

12. Hamner, *Short Grass*, 194.

13. William M. Pearce, *The Matador Land and Cattle Company* (Norman: University of Oklahoma Press, 1964), 7.

14. W. G. Kerr, *Scottish Capital on the American Credit Frontier* (Austin: Texas State Historical Association, 1976), 44–45.

15. Marisue Burleson Potts, *Motley County Roundup: Over 100 Years of Gathering in Texas,* 2nd ed. (Matador: Mollie Burleson Ranch Ltd., 2020), 133–35.

16. Pearce, *Matador*, 28.

17. Murdo Mackenzie, interview by J. Evetts Haley, November 22,1932, as cited in J. Evetts Haley, *Charles Goodnight: Cowman and Plainsman,* new ed. (1936; Norman: University of Oklahoma Press, 1949), 350.

18. Ibid., as cited in Pearce, *Matador*, 40.

19. Potts, *Motley County Roundup,* 136–40.

20. Haley, *Goodnight,* 126–27.

21. Ibid., 121–22.

22. This original chuck-box is preserved by the Panhandle-Plains Historical Society at Canyon, Texas.

23. After the US Army defeated the Mescalero Apaches and Diné (Navajo People) in western New Mexico Territory in 1863, Navajos were forced to walk over 350 miles to a reservation in east-central New Mexico. Known by the Navajos as the "Long Walk," they made the difficult journey, often in chilling cold or stifling heat, in several groups. The Navajo continued to arrive at Bosque Redondo Indian Reservation for a period of over two years. At its peak in the winter of 1864, more than 8,500 Navajo and nearly 500 Mescalero Apache people were held there. The US Army began regular supply caravans to Bosque Redondo via the Cimarron Branch of the Santa Fe Trail in 1863, but by 1864 a more direct route across the Texas Panhandle shaved 100 miles off the trip. Freighters hauled flour, wheat, and corn on the trail, and cattlemen such as Goodnight drove cattle there to feed the Navajos and Mescaleros until 1868, when they were allowed to return home.

24. Haley, *Goodnight*, 140.

25. Ibid., 295–96.

26. Harley True Burton, *A History of the J A Ranch* (Austin: Von Boeckmann-Jones Company, 1928): 22–23.

27. Haley, *Goodnight*, 301–302.

28. Ibid., 351.

29. Walsh resigned from the JA to take a position with the Brazil Land, Cattle, and Packing Company, managed by Murdo Mackenzie, then moved on to Rhodesia, where he took charge of the ranching interests of the British South African Company.

30. Burton, *History of the J A*, 109–10.

31. Ibid., 123–24. For a complete menu of the 1927 dinner, see Burton's footnote 8.

32. Ibid., 124.

33. Ibid., 128.

34. Ibid., 116.

35. Lynn R. Bailey, *"We'll All Wear Silk Hats": The Erie and Chiricahua Cattle Companies and the Rise of Corporate Ranching in the Sulphur Spring Valley of Arizona, 1883–1999* (Tucson: Westernlore Press, 1994), viii–x.

36. Ibid., 71–80.

37. Ibid., 120–23.

38. Ibid., 177–78.

39. Ibid., 179.

40. Ibid., 182.

41. Diana Hadley, et al., *El Rio Bonito: An Ethnoecological Study of the Bonita Creek Watershed* (Phoenix: Arizona State Office of the Bureau of Land Management, 1993), 219–20. Hampson owned the Mexico, Cuernavaca, and Pacific Railway.

42. Frank M. King, *Pioneer Western Empire Builders* (Pasadena: Trail's End Publishing Company, 1946), 197.

43. Ibid., 291–92.

44. J. Evetts Haley, *Jeff Milton: A Good Man with a Gun* (Norman: University of Oklahoma Press, 1948), 136.

45. Ibid., 300.

46. "Who Were the Real War Horses of WWI?," BBC, http://www.bbc.co.uk/guides/zp6bjxs; and "American Horses, Mules Joined Soldiers in WWI," *The Horse,* accessed April 23, 2018, https://thehorse.com/110055/american-horses-mules-joined-soldiers-in-wwi/.

47. Brigadier-General T. R. F. Bate, "Buying British Remounts in America," in *The Horse and The War,* Captain Sidney Galtrey (London: Country Life, 1918; reprint, LaVergne, TN: Kessinger Publishing, 2010), 27.

48. "Horses and World War I," Ypres Peace Monument, Stories and Facts, accessed April 23, 2018, http://www.yprespeacemonument.com/horses-and-wwi/.

49. *Final Report of General John J. Pershing, Commander-in-Chief American Expeditionary Forces* (Washington, DC: Government Printing Office, 1920), 70–71.

50. Robert H. Ferrell, *America's Deadliest Battle: Meuse-Argonne, 1918* (Lawrence: University Press of Kansas, 2007), 4–5.

51. *Final Report,* 71.

52. Ferrell, *America's Deadliest Battle,* 4–5.

53. Saje Mathieu, "Lafayette, We Are Here," (lecture, National World War I Museum and Memorial 2017 Symposium, Kansas City, MO, November 3, 2017).

54. "Army Horse Care in the First World War," National Army Museum, Horses, accessed April 23, 2018, https://www.nam.ac.uk/explore/british-army-horses-during-first-world-war.

55. Richard S. Faulkner, *The School of Hard Knocks: Combat Leadership in the American Expeditionary Forces* (College Station: Texas A&M University Press, 2012), 149.

56. "Congress Passes Draft Bill by Big Majority," *Amarillo Daily News,* April 29, 1917.

57. "Texas' Total Quota Under First Draft To Be 30,545 Men," *Houston Post,* July 26, 1917.

58. *US, World War I Draft Registration Cards, 1917–1918* (database), Ancestry.com, Provo, UT: Ancestry.com Operations Inc., 2005, accessed February 3, 2022.

59. Major George Wythe, *A History of the 90th Division* (New York: The 90th Division Association, 1920), 162.

60. Ibid., 164.

61. Uniformed sentinels did not appear at the Tomb until 1926, and they did not begin guarding the site twenty-four hours a day until 1937. The sarcophagus was not erected until 1932.

62. He also produced a *Spirit of the American Navy,* but few of those exist. They are located at Kingman, AZ; Clearwater, and Palatka ("Sailor"), FL; Naperville, IL; Fort Wayne, IN; Granite and Hobart, OK; and Crowell, TX. The example at Crowell is carved in stone.

INDEX

Note: Page numbers in *italics* denote images and associated captions.